BREAKING CASUALTY COVENANTS

REALIZING THE WEIGHT OF YOUR WORDS

by
Mickie Winborn

Harrison House
Tulsa, Oklahoma

Breaking Casualty Covenants
—Realizing the Weight of Your Words
ISBN 1-57794-267-1
Copyright © 2000 by Mickie Winborn
P.O. Box 19194
Houston, TX 77024

Published by Harrison House, Inc.
P.O. Box 35035
Tulsa, Oklahoma 74153

DEDICATION

This book is dedicated to my family: First, to my husband, who patiently accepted my commitment to produce it. Next, to my granddaughter, Tracy, and to my grandson, Kelly, for their clerical assistance and great suggestions. And to my beautiful daughters-in-law, Amber and Karen, for their time and love in helping to bring it all together.

Special thanks go to Quin Sherrer, an accomplished author who gave me sure guidance from her wealth of writing experience.

Also, thank you to the college students who did research, organized and proofread material and blessed me when they said that they received personal help from reading the text.

Lastly, this book is dedicated to all who shared their own stories about casualty covenants and to those who have steadfastly prayed that it would benefit all who read it. Without their love and support, this book would not have been possible.

CONTENTS

There is a plan of prosperity for each one of us. This book opens your eyes to agreements you have made that will produce decrease in your life. As you read, you will find strategies of increase coming into your mind. Mickie Winborn has a winner in this book.

The principles in this book will cause you to be victorious!

Charles D. Pierce
Vice President, Global Harvest Ministries
Glory of Zion International Ministries

FOREWORD

The power of choice is phenomenal—choices by human beings affect human lives!

This simple word, *choice,* is the backdrop of Mickie Winborn's book, *Breaking Casualty Covenants,* and it is something that compels us to look at the scope of life now and in the hereafter through its lens.

Choices draw us into decisions, and decisions determine direction and outcome. The key question is, *What should we know in order to press toward the very best decisions day by day, and can anything be done if we miss the mark?*

The bounty of information shared in this book about life choices addresses these issues in a truly sensible, God-ordained manner.

Mickie Winborn writes succinctly. Her book speaks with conviction about how much God longs for us to embrace and sustain a productive covenant relationship with Him and to resist any "casualty covenant" partnership with Satan, our archenemy.

Each individual faces life with the challenge of confronting his sin nature and the snares set by Satan for his destruction; but it is also true that each individual faces life with available gifts from God to impact our choices for good. This book helps us distinguish various dimensions of privilege and opportunity by using God's Word as the foundational plumb line.

Human choices cannot change the sovereignty of God, but they can change human destinies. By human choice we cannot decrease the import of God's wisdom or alter the power of His love. The wonder of it all is how God reaches out from His sovereignty to offer man a holy choice, a divine plan of mercy and rescue, a consistent goodness and loving helpfulness as revealed in Jesus Christ, His Son.

John 3:16 speaks of this holy choice on God's part to love and forgive, and Psalm 139:13-18 TLB speaks of this choice on God's part to daily express that love. The challenge is in comprehending this trustworthy love and in knowing that every choice for our lives can be determined in the light of this amazing gift. This is the "perfect love" with power to cast out all entanglements of demonic fear (1 John 4:18), no matter what circumstance or choice we face. What privilege; what opportunity!

Christ Himself, while living here on earth, modeled the wonder of this privilege and opportunity. He submitted everything to God in prayer, waited for His answers and acted by His power. (John 5:30 AMP.)

Proverbs 2:6,9-10 TLB states how this provision of grace is available to us: *For the Lord grants wisdom! His every word is a treasure of knowledge and understanding.... He shows how to distinguish right from wrong, how to find the right decision every time. For wisdom and truth will enter the very center of your being, filling your life with joy.*

My dear friend Mickie has consistently chosen to receive this provision personally. Her own life experiences have been a unique school of revelation in matters of spiritual discernment, study and choice. That is why I rejoice in her wonderful, biblical presentation of the power of choice. She makes it so clear—the truth that only God has the best answers but that He will wait for our partnership with Him in order to make His best answers our final choice.

—Barbara James
World Intercession Network

Casualty Covenant:

A conscious or unconscious agreement
made with forces of darkness
that may lead to bondage, distress,
disease or death.

INTRODUCTION

Breaking Casualty Covenants is written to answer people's questions regarding why bad things often happen to good people. Once your understanding is opened in this matter, you will be much less likely to continually "shoot yourself in the foot" and then wonder why you are wounded.

You see, as we race along our innermost tracks of mental conflicts and emotional hang-ups, too often we make bad decisions and faulty judgments. These self-defeating decisions and judgments can eternally affect our lives and the lives of others as we unknowingly, carelessly or mistakenly make a covenant, or an agreement, with a spirit of darkness. The truth is, we are often the main cause of the "casualties" we suffer in life.

Even Christians can be ensnared by this devilish device of casualty agreements. You may ask, "Can a Christian who understands how to trust God's Word still make agreements with the deceiver?" Yes, he can, because God gives him free will to choose.

God is sovereign, but He has chosen to limit Himself to our choices. That's why Joshua 24:15 RSV says, **Choose this day whom you will serve.** And Psalm 78:41 says, **Yea, they turned back and tempted God, and *limited* the Holy One of Israel.** That's also why our enemy, Satan, uses dirty tricks to bring us into agreement

11

with him. Even the most dedicated believers can be ensnared by his deceitful schemes and caused to make wrong choices.

But there is a way out! You yourself can break any covenants you have unknowingly made with the enemy that have kept you in bondage. This book will ring a loud wake-up bell in the recesses of your memory to reveal any agreements you have made in the past that lead to death instead of life. It will then help you break any casualty covenants you're making or are about to make concerning your relationships, your health, your finances or your future.

I also want to show you how to break any curses that have kept you bound and replace them with the truth that sets you free. Obviously, just as blessings can be passed from one generation to the next, so can curses. These are often called *inheritance curses*.

You may observe an inheritance curse as a genetic, predisposed family pattern that is set in motion by parents or grandparents. That pattern may appear as learned behavior. But although the assumption that certain patterns are learned behavior carries some validity, the deeper root lies in an inheritance curse that has to be broken.

These generational curses seem to run in the family bloodline. Family members often don't know the activities of their ancestors; therefore, curses can unknowingly be passed on to third and fourth generations. (Ex. 20:5.)

For example, if you become involved in any way with the realm of the occult, you can bring curses upon yourself and your descendants. These curses are often the consequence of seeking knowledge from ungodly sources, including fortunetelling, sorcery, astrology, witchcraft and necromancy, which is any type of communication with the dead (it is actually consulting with an evil familiar spirit counterfeiting the deceased, according to Deuteronomy 18:10-12). *However, the Holy Spirit can help you break ancestral curses.*

My previous book, *Through a Glass, Darkly,* briefly mentions this extraordinary phenomenon of breaking agreements that do not lead to life. The majority of that book deals with the story of my deliverance when I was miraculously healed of terminal ovarian cancer many years ago. Throughout that trying time, by the grace of God I received deep insight and understanding of the negative effects caused by ignorantly making covenants with the devil.

God Almighty has miraculously healed and delivered many who have read *Through a Glass, Darkly* and then acted on what they've learned. These people have been set free as they've broken their covenants with premature death, disease, financial lack and other seemingly insurmountable problems, choosing instead to agree with God's Word.

My prayer as I wrote *Breaking Casualty Covenants* was that the truths I more fully disclose will set many more free from the bondage of casualty covenants and help lead them to the abundant blessings that come from knowing and believing the Word of God.

—*Mickie Winborn*

1

WHAT ARE
CASUALTY COVENANTS?

Most of us have to make decisions every day. To ensure that we make wise decisions, we must stay flexible, because people, seasons and circumstances are in a constant state of change.

However, we can be sure of one thing—the Word of God *never* changes. First Peter 1:25 says, **The word of the Lord endureth *for ever.*** Therefore, if we want to receive the benefits God has in store for us in this life, we must rely on His truth to constantly guide us in making both minor and major decisions.

Sadly, many fail to seek God for wisdom in the choices they make. Instead, people in desperate situations often make desperate decisions. But the consequences are grave when people make ungodly decisions that violate the Word of God. Sometimes their unwise choices lead to the destruction of marriages, relationships, families, careers and even life itself.

Others constantly make wrong decisions based on their faulty personal belief systems rather than on God's guidance. These people think their emotions and decision-making processes are under their own private control. But in truth, both their conscious and unconscious decisions become *casualty covenants* with the enemy, resulting in the negative outcomes they have come to expect.

A casualty covenant is a conscious or unconscious agreement made with forces of darkness that may lead to bondage, distress, disease or death. The dictionary defines the word *covenant* as "a binding and solemn agreement to do or keep from doing a specific thing."[1] This type of demonic agreement is indeed binding, for it is strong enough to change the course of a person's life.

These subconscious, or subliminal, agreements that exist in the mind and emotions can affect our thoughts and behavior without our conscious awareness. Temptations come first to our mind through our thoughts. We need to be on guard that we do not give an opportunity for evil spirits to invade our thought life: **Neither give place to the devil,** Ephesians 4:27 says.

CHOICES THAT LEAD TO LIFE OR DEATH
. . .

It is evident that the father of lies—Satan himself—tries regularly to infiltrate our thought lives. His carefully engineered suggestions and strategies are designed to bring death not only to our dreams but to our bodies as quickly as possible!

Psychiatrists are well aware that we humans can make unconscious decisions and judgments that bring about either delight or disaster in our lives. They call these "self-fulfilling prophecies." Psychiatrists are also familiar with death wishes that open the door in many people's lives to a *spirit* of death.

First Kings 17:10-15 is a Bible story that illustrates the power of making the right choice between life and death. A widow of the town of Zarephath told the prophet Elijah, "I have only a little food to cook for me and my son, that we may eat it and die."

This occurred during a time of great drought and famine, and by her words this woman had already made a covenant to die of starvation. However, she broke that covenant when she trusted in the word of the Lord prophesied through Elijah, that God would supernaturally provide ample food for her and her son. That word came to pass because the woman made a choice that led to life instead of death.

It is interesting to note that when the mother broke her covenant with death, the son was set free from starvation at the same time.

CASUALTY COVENANTS AFFECT OUR HEALTH
• • •

One area in our lives that these covenants can affect is our health. For instance, you have probably heard people say things like, "All the men in my family died of heart attacks, so I probably will too."

Christians are not immune to accepting this lie of the enemy. If their relatives suffer or even die from a particular disease, they may become vulnerable to the suggestion that they will contract the same illness. Too often they forget that the God who created DNA also knows how to fix it! After all, Jesus said that whatever we ask believing, we will receive. (Mark 11:24.)

Believing in our hearts and saying with our mouths that we might develop certain diseases fulfills a biblical principle in a negative way. From our hearts, we are speaking what we believe will come to pass; and, therefore, we will have what we say.

And Jesus, replying, said to them, Have faith in God [constantly]. Truly I tell you, whoever says to this mountain, Be lifted up and thrown into the sea! and does not doubt at all in his heart but believes that what he says will take place, it will be done for him.

Mark 11:22,23 AMP

So that verse also works for the negative. Satan is a thief who has come to rob us of life. He uses the leverage of an inheritance curse or a so-called genetic disease to persuade us to agree with his lies by speaking and believing them. If we allow that kind of satanic input to dominate our thought life, it becomes easy to make an agreement, a casualty covenant, with our deadly foe, accepting distress or disease as inevitable.

Satan likes it when we are in this vulnerable state, so he tries to keep us either ignorant of or disobedient to God's Word. When we lack knowledge of God's Word or are disobedient to its truth, we are like open targets in a pitching booth at the county fair: we can be hit by one of the devil's balls of fire and never know what happened!

Only by understanding and obeying God's Word will we avoid being defeated by the devil. When we don't obey the Word of God, we are in rebellion whether we know it or not—and 1 Samuel 15:23 says, **Rebellion is as the sin of witchcraft, and stubbornness is as iniquity and idolatry.** The fact is, disobedience sets us up for disaster.

On the other hand, Jesus said that knowing God's truth sets people free. (John 8:32.) And according to 1 Timothy 2:3-4, this is God's will for *all* men:

> **For this is good and acceptable in the sight of God our Saviour; who will have all men to be saved, and to come unto the knowledge of the truth.**

THE BITTER FRUIT OF WRONG COVENANTS
* * *

Strongholds of bitterness, anger and unforgiveness in our hearts can also tempt us into making wrong covenants, causing casualties in our lives and in the lives of those around us. These casualty covenants don't always come from words we speak. Sometimes our thought life or our emotions can trigger them.

Damaged emotions often cause people to develop poor judgment. I had an acquaintance who is a good example of this. The man was a war hero who had served his country well. Later, when working in the business world, he also served his company well.

But when this man's company merged with another company, he was not promoted as he had expected to be. He became bitter about it, unconsciously making a covenant with a spirit of bitterness.

This man remained in that bitter state and eventually became an alcoholic. He resisted help from family and friends and later died from complications due to the alcohol. His widow became bitter, too, saying that his friends had let him down.

You see, bitterness is contagious. Hebrews 12:15 AMP warns us that bitterness can defile others.

Exercise foresight and be on the watch to look [after one another], to see that no one falls back from and fails to secure God's grace (His unmerited favor and spiritual blessing), in order that no root of resentment (rancor, bitterness, or hatred) shoots forth and causes trouble and bitter torment, and the many become contaminated and defiled by it.

CASUALTY COVENANTS AFFECT OUR FINANCES
• • •

Oftentimes people make similar covenants that negatively affect their financial lives. For example, some say, "I'm poor. I've always been poor. I will always be poor." These people may not realize it, but they are making a covenant with the enemy to stay poor—a covenant that only they can break.

Now, most of us understand that a person receives no wages if he doesn't work. The apostle Paul said it succinctly: **If any would not work, neither should he eat** (2 Thess. 3:10). Of course, we don't expect those who are seriously ill or handicapped to work; however, even these people may need to assist in taking care of themselves.

Jesus said that the poor will always be among us and that we are to provide for them. (Matt. 26:11.) As one minister said, "Instead of working to *get*, we should work to *give*."

Paul reminds us in Acts 20:35 that there is joy in having enough to be able to give to others.

> **I have shewed you all things, how that so labouring ye ought to support the weak, and to remember the words of the Lord Jesus, how he said, *It is more blessed to give than to receive*.**

Our ultimate source is not our salary; it is Jehovah Jireh, our provider. Abraham used this compound name of God in Genesis 22:14 when God provided a ram for him to sacrifice as a burnt offering. God is still the same today. He is the God who provides for all our needs:

> **And my God will liberally supply (fill to the full) your every need according to His riches in glory in Christ Jesus.**
>
> **Philippians 4:19 AMP**

However, God cannot pour out His abundance on those who agree with the enemy regarding their finances. Remember, Mark 11:24 says, **Therefore I say unto you, what things soever ye desire, when ye pray, *believe that ye receive them*, and ye shall have them.**

It is a fact that Christians often pray and then doubt that they will receive anything. This is praying without faith, and according to Hebrews 11:6, it produces no results:

> **Without faith it is impossible to please him: for he that cometh to God must believe that he is, and that he is a rewarder of them that diligently seek him.**

Our Words Can Bless or Curse

• • •

The devil continually searches for a doorway into our thought life so he can trick us into agreeing with him. And he plays dirty! For instance, he accuses us falsely, according to Revelation 12:10: **The accuser of our brethren...accused them before our God day and night.** He even uses others who are close to us to plant his lies in our minds.

Let me show you what I mean. You may be familiar with the saying, "Sticks and stones may break my bones, but words will never hurt me." Well, the following account proves that words can hurt—a lot!

Several years ago, I was in San José, Costa Rica, ministering in different churches around the city. At every meeting, God Almighty confirmed His Word with signs and wonders.

The joy that one experiences in the presence of the risen, healing Jesus is contagious. We saw manifested miracles right before our eyes as pain left and bodies were healed in an instant!

At one particular Women's Aglow International meeting, I was impressed to share an exposé of the devil's dangerous device of casualty covenants. I also felt led to teach on how one can break such covenants. The audience listened intently. Suddenly, a woman stood up and hastily left the room. I was still speaking when she returned.

The woman interrupted me, asking, "Can I tell what just happened to me?" Her face radiated pure joy as she related to us what had just happened:

22

I listened to Mickie talking about casualty covenants. Then she said that we needed to ask the Holy Spirit to reveal to us whether or not we had ever made a casualty covenant about anything or anyone.

As I prayed, I immediately remembered how fast I had grown as a child. I was taller than any of my classmates. Because this made me self-conscious, I began to slump in my posture. My mother would tell me, "If you don't quit slumping, someday you will have a hump on your back."

I would temporarily straighten up, but my consciousness of my height would cause me to start drooping in posture again. Mother would repeat over and over, "If you don't quit slumping, someday you will have a hump on your back." Finally, I resigned myself to developing a hump on my back just as my mother said I would.

Today as I listened to Mickie and then prayed, I understood for the first time why a hump had formed on my back. Years ago I had agreed with my mother's words—and what I believed for eventually came to pass!

So I left this meeting, went to the ladies' room and removed the upper part of my clothing. Looking at the hump, I said, "In the name of Jesus Christ, I break my covenant with you, Satan, that I will have a hump on my back. That covenant is broken forever!" Right before my eyes, the hump disappeared! I witnessed a miracle!

Spontaneous joy erupted with thanksgiving to God all over the room. We had a joyous time celebrating that woman's victory!

This illustration demonstrates the power in the words we speak. Our words can heal, or they can hurt. They can bless, or they can curse! James 3:6 puts it this way:

The tongue is a fire, a world of iniquity: so is the tongue among our members, that it defileth the whole body, and setteth on

**fire the course of nature; and it is set on
fire of hell.**

That woman's mother meant her words for good, but
they imposed a verbal curse upon her daughter. In a
similar way, impatience, anger and frustration can cause
a person to utter words that wound another. These
wounds can become a curse in that person's life,
adversely affecting him for years or even a lifetime.

BREAKING WRONG COVENANTS
THROUGH OUR COVENANT WITH GOD
• • •

Self-imposed curses on our lives have to be revoked
if we are to be free of them. We also need to pray for
God's restoration in the areas of our lives in which curses
have done their damage.

The good news is that Jesus became a curse so we
might receive His blessing and be freed from the curse.
Through His sacrifice on the Cross, He made provision
for our deliverance from all curses.

> **Christ purchased our freedom [redeem-
> ing us] from the curse (doom) of the Law
> [and its condemnation] by [Himself] becom-
> ing a curse for us, for it is written [in the
> Scriptures], Cursed is everyone who hangs
> on a tree (is crucified).**

Galatians 3:13 AMP

Now we walk in covenant relationship with Almighty
God Himself. That covenant is called the Abrahamic
Covenant because God first established it with Abraham.
(Gen. 17:7.).

As believers, we are counted as Abraham's seed and can therefore claim the blessings according to Galatians 4:28: **Now we, brethren, as Isaac was, are the children of promise.** Acts 3:25 also refers to the blessings we have inherited through the Abrahamic covenant:

> **Ye are the children of the prophets, and of the covenant which God made with our fathers, saying unto Abraham, And in thy seed shall all the kindreds of the earth be blessed.**

The Old Testament contains the covenant God established with Abraham, and the New Testament contains our covenant through Jesus Christ. The old covenant was sealed by circumcision of the flesh. However, the new covenant is sealed by circumcision of the *heart*, which is accomplished as our spirits are born again. (Rom. 2:28,29.)

Philippians 3:3 AMP talks about this spiritual circumcision:

> **For we** [Christians] **are the true circumcision, who worship God in spirit and by the Spirit of God and exult and glory and pride ourselves in Jesus Christ.**

The New Testament describes the covenant that God the Father cut with His sinless Son Jesus. Jesus provided a covenant of grace through the shedding of His righteous blood.

Many noble parents are willing to sacrifice their lives for their children's sake. But Jesus Christ is the only perfect sacrifice before a holy God because He is the only One completely without sin.

Because of Jesus' sacrifice, now anyone can enter into the new covenant. Romans 10:9-13 explains how:

If thou shalt confess with thy mouth the Lord Jesus, and shalt believe in thine heart that God hath raised him from the dead, thou shalt be saved. For with the heart man believeth unto righteousness; and with the mouth confession is made unto salvation.

For the scripture saith, Whosoever believeth on him shall not be ashamed. For there is no difference between the Jew and the Greek: for the same Lord over all is rich unto all that call upon him. For whosoever shall call upon the name of the Lord shall be saved.

Finally, Psalm 111:9 assures us that eternal redemption is ours when we enter into covenant with God: **He sent redemption unto his people:** *he hath commanded his covenant for ever:* **holy and reverend is his name.** As children of God, we are covenant people—forever!

So don't delay! If you haven't already received Jesus as your Savior, decide now to enter into covenant with Him. Receive Him today by inviting Him into your heart. The moment you do that, His Holy Spirit enters your eternal spirit and your spirit is born again. This new life contains the holy nature of Jesus Christ and the ability to live free from the bondage of all the wrong covenants you have made in the past.

FREEDOM FROM EVERY CURSE

We know that Jesus Christ died for all humanity. Yet many are not saved because they have not personally appropriated this truth or laid claim to it for themselves as their right.

Unfortunately, the same principle applies to many of us who are children of God. Often we remain under certain curses of the law because we have not appropriated Jesus' redemptive work of becoming a curse for us. Only the truth we believe *and* receive brings liberty.

Disobedience to God can also result in a curse on our lives. In fact, the Bible mentions more than seventy curses that come as a result of disobedience to God's Word! (Deut. 27:15-26; 28:15-45.) Our parent's and grandparent's disobedience can bring an inheritance curse upon us as well.

Therefore, it is up to us to apply scriptural principles and break any curses from ourselves and our family members. Second Chronicles 7:14 provides one of those principles:

If my people, which are called by my name, shall humble themselves, and pray, and seek my face, and turn from their wicked ways; then will I hear from heaven, and will forgive their sin, and will heal their land.

God's will for us is to enjoy abundant life. Jesus said, **I came so they can have real and eternal life, more and better life than they ever dreamed of** (John 10:10 THE MESSAGE).

Psalm 84:11-12 tells us just how much God wants to do for us:

For the Lord God is a sun and shield: the Lord will give grace and glory: *no good*

***thing will he withhold from them that walk
uprightly. O Lord of hosts, blessed is the
man that trusteth in thee.***

Most of us suffer occasionally from attacks of
negative emotions such as self-pity, fear, rejection and
bitterness. Satan's plan is always to deceive through
these emotions—to make something wrong seem right.

We can't keep these transient attacks from coming to
our thoughts. But just as we don't have to let birds that fly
over our heads make a nest in our hair, we also don't
have to dwell on those negative emotions. As we come
to understand this device of the devil to deceive us into
making covenants with him, we can then cut his evil
influence out of our thoughts and decisions.

ONE WOMAN'S TESTIMONY
• • •

Jacquelyn Sheppard, a Christian leader and mother
of three children, is an example of someone who made a
casualty covenant with the enemy that almost cost her
life. In her case, the enemy used an onslaught of arrows
of accusation regarding her relationship with her family
to deceive her.

Jacquelyn and her husband, Glenn, founded International Prayer Ministries. Glenn frequently traveled for the
ministry, often keeping him away from home for long
periods of time. Because of this, Jacquelyn assumed more
and more responsibility for their home and three children.

In addition, Jacquelyn founded a private high school
for Christian students. Once the doors to this facility
opened, the results were incredible! Students gave up

drugs, illicit sex and devious activities. Jacquelyn worked sixteen to eighteen hours a day, in addition to counseling special cases on Saturday and Sunday afternoons.

Meanwhile, she kept seeking qualified workers. Although the school was successful, Jacquelyn could not keep dedicated help. Frustrated with this chronic lack of responsible employees, Jacquelyn began to murmur, "Why can't these people see the urgency of this work?" She realized that most people were afraid to work with teenagers. But the need was so great; she yearned for people who would put their hearts and hands to the task.

The longer this stressful situation continued, the more Jacquelyn struggled with an array of negative emotions. She felt betrayed by those in spiritual leadership around her. It seemed that like Uriah—the Old Testament soldier whom King David betrayed in battle—she had been led into battle, only to have those around her pull away and leave her to fight alone. (2 Sam. 11:15.) She also felt as if the harvest of souls were rotting in the field and she couldn't get the body of Christ around her to see it. The people just weren't there to help.

The spiritual attack was fierce as accusing thoughts concerning her family and friends bombarded Jacquelyn's mind. The devil had come to stop her, but first he had to convince her to agree with all of his lying accusations.

This is a common strategy of the devil, because lying and deceiving is an essential part of his nature.

He was a murderer from the beginning and does not stand in the truth, because there is no truth in him. When he speaks a falsehood, he speaks what is natural to him,

**for he is a liar [himself] and the father of lies
and of all that is false.**

John 8:44 AMP

Looking back, Jacquelyn recalled how the enemy plotted her destruction. His strategy was to ensnare her by deception. First he attacked her mind with accusing thoughts about those who had failed to help her with the school. Then he worked on her thought life, telling her the lie that she would die prematurely from cancer until she finally agreed, or made a covenant, with him to accept that lie as inevitable.

Satan knew that Jacquelyn's Father God would not violate her personal decision, because He gives everyone the freedom to make his or her own choices. *God did not create robots.* God's Spirit never interferes with a person's free will.

Jacquelyn had been able to hear from the Lord since she was a child. As a wife and mother, she had assumed the responsibility to hear His words for her husband and children. Jacquelyn recalled how the enemy used this practice to accuse her of three things:

First, because I usually heard from the Lord and told my family what I heard, the enemy accused me of interfering in my family's ability to seek a word from the Lord for themselves. Second, he said that because I delivered the Lord's word to them, I was keeping them from their own personal spiritual growth. And finally, he said that if I were to shut up, my family would grow closer to the Lord.

To give up hearing from the Lord would be death to me. But those were the lies I accepted.

So Satan waged war in Jacquelyn's thoughts against two of the most precious things in her life: hearing God's voice and her family's spiritual growth.

At this point, Satan's strategy had worked. He had deceived Jacquelyn into believing that the Father God wanted to take her home to heaven so He could minister personally to her family. The moment she accepted that lie as God's will for her, she unknowingly entered into a hidden agreement with the devil. She made a covenant with his lies that would cause her to become a casualty.

The enemy had threatened Jacquelyn with death four years earlier. At the time, she was gaining ground in battling Satan regarding some of her students' occult practices. She explained:

> I told Satan then that he couldn't take my life, because I belonged to Jesus. So later he tried to trick me with a new tactic: He sought to deceive me into making a casualty covenant with him so that I would, in essence, bring about my own death.

Jacquelyn began her encounter with death after a routine mammogram revealed a tumor in her breast. Her friends expected God to heal her. When the healing didn't occur, many misunderstood and stopped praying for her. Many of the young people to whom she had ministered couldn't understand why God would let her have cancer. Because of this, some fell back into sin, and Jacquelyn grieved with a wounded heart.

> For the next ten months, I continued to wait before the Lord, reading the Word and books that described the struggles of others who had faced the "dark night of the soul." I knew God was there; I just couldn't determine what He was doing. Finally, I came to the point where I said to the Lord, "If I never hear Your voice again, I still have to follow after

You. And as best I can, even if You never speak to me again, I will do what I think You would have me do."

Jacquelyn's condition worsened. One day her friend Barbara James called her. Barbara and her husband, Bane, founders of Joysprings Foundation, Inc., were holding a retreat with other prayer intercessors in Franklin Springs, Georgia. I was one of those invited to attend. Barbara also urged Jacquelyn to come to the retreat, but Jacquelyn told her that she didn't have enough physical strength to attend.

Soon afterwards, however, the Lord gave Jacquelyn a dream. In her dream, Barbara James walked into her room and said, "Jackie will be here in the morning at 10:45." Immediately upon waking, Jacquelyn knew the Lord wanted her to attend the retreat. So with little strength but much determination, she got in the car and drove to Franklin Springs.

It was at this retreat, while basking in an atmosphere of God's power and love, that Jacquelyn received her first indication of a miraculous healing taking place. Chuck Pierce, founder of Glory of Zion Ministry and Vice President of Global Harvest, was impressed by the Lord to break the power of word curses spoken over Jacquelyn. Then the Holy Spirit impressed me to kneel at her feet and lay hands on her for healing, according to Mark 16:18: **They shall lay hands on the sick, and they shall recover.**

The following is Jacquelyn's description of the prayer meeting:

> A few precious intercessor friends of mine began to pray, breaking the power of wrong words that had been

spoken against me. I felt something in the spiritual realm leave me.

Later that evening, Mickie gently began to teach me what a "casualty covenant" was. As I listened, I realized that two-and-a-half months before the cancer, I had unwittingly entered into that kind of agreement through the deception of the enemy. Mickie then led me through the process of breaking the unconscious covenant I had made with death. I believe that for healing to manifest in my physical body, that covenant first had to be broken.

Satan had a plan to destroy, but God had a better plan to restore!

By His Spirit of Truth, God led Jacquelyn to a place of refuge and comfort, where He ministered help to her through His servants. When she broke her covenant with death in the name of Jesus Christ, she was immediately set free from an evil spirit of death.

Today, Jacquelyn once again ministers life to others. She and her husband are back on the front lines of the army of the Lord God of Hosts, serving Him with renewed vigor.

Learn a lesson from Jacquelyn's testimony. You must protect yourself from the specific danger of making a covenant with death. Don't become a casualty!

2

OPENING THE DOOR

As you consider the possibility that you may have made casualty covenants with the enemy at some time in your past, your first response may be disbelief. "I would never agree with Satan about anything!" you may protest. But remember, Satan is a master of deception.

Most of us know that the devil comes to steal, to kill and to destroy. (John 10:10.) We also know that he is like a poisonous snake that we don't want anywhere near us or our loved ones.

However, if we are ignorant of Satan's deceptive devices, we can unknowingly open a door into our thought life, allowing him to sneak into our patterns of thinking. This permits him access to our decision-making processes. Therefore, we must always stay on guard, **lest Satan should get an advantage of us: for we are not ignorant of his devices** (2 Cor. 2:11).

For instance, have you ever made statements such as, "I knew it was never going to work out!" or "I had hoped it would happen, but I knew it wouldn't"? These are the kinds of thoughts that can lead to casualty covenants.

THE FIRST DECEPTION
. . .

Scripture tells us that the serpent in the Garden of Eden was inhabited by Satan, who was more subtle than any beast of the field the Lord God had made. (Gen. 3:1.) Revelation 12:9 gives us more insight about the devil:

And the great dragon was cast out, that old serpent, called the Devil, and Satan, which deceiveth the whole world: he was cast out into the earth, and his angels were cast out with him.

This sly, crafty, tricky, wicked fallen angel has one primary goal: to deceive and lead astray as many as he can from the truth.

He started out by deceiving Eve in the Garden of Eden. Then he convinced Adam to disobey as well.

Adam was created with amazing intelligence. As all the created animals paraded before him, he evaluated each one's appearance and appropriately named them. Yet with all of Adam's intelligence, he still joined Eve in disobedience to the Creator. His intellectual ability did not keep him from making a very foolish decision!

Someone once said, "It wasn't the *pear* in the tree that caused all the problems. It was the *pair* on the ground!"

Since Adam and Eve, the devil has continued to find ways to deceive mankind. One of his favorite strategies over the centuries has been to use the world's system to lead people down the road of deception.

For instance, he tries to brainwash us into believing we can become our own salvation. The world says, "If it feels good, do it." But what feels good to our senses and our inherited sin nature is most often in direct conflict with our Creator's good will for our lives.

GOD WANTS US *WHOLE*—SPIRIT, SOUL AND BODY

You see, we are made up of three distinct parts: spirit, soul and body. And God wants to bless us *wholly* in all three realms of our beings. That's why it is so important that we break casualty covenants we may have made in any area of our lives, for each of these wrong covenants hinders us from receiving God's blessings.

We can clearly see from the following Scriptures that spirit, soul and body are separate parts of our beings.

And the very God of peace sanctify you wholly; and I pray God your whole *spirit and soul and body* be preserved blameless unto the coming of our Lord Jesus Christ.

1 Thessalonians 5:23

For the word of God is quick, and powerful, and sharper than any two-edged sword, piercing even to the dividing asunder of soul and spirit, and of the joints and marrow, and is a discerner of the thoughts and intents of the heart.

Hebrews 4:12

Unlike any other created being, man's being is a "trinity," having been given the ability to communicate on three levels:

- Because man is a spirit, he is capable of *God-consciousness* and communion with God. (Job 32:8; Ps. 18:28; Prov. 20:27.)

- Because man has a soul, he has *self-consciousness.* (Ps. 13:2; 42:5,6,11.)

- Because man lives in a body, he has, through his senses, *world-consciousness.* (Gen. 1:26.)[1]

THE HUMAN SPIRIT
. . .

Now, let's explore this more closely. First, man's human *spirit* is the eternal part of that trinity that is re-created at the moment of salvation.

By a choice of our will, we believe with our hearts and confess with our mouths that Jesus Christ is the Son of God, that He died on the Cross for our sins and arose from the grave on the third day. At the moment of confessing this truth with faith in our hearts, we are born again. (Rom. 10:9,10.) Instantly we receive a divine infusion as the Holy Spirit enters our human spirits to take up residence.

In essence, we undergo a heart transplant! We become new creatures in Christ! Suddenly we're able to partake of His divine nature and life. We are accepted into the family of God. Angels rejoice! Our friends and families wonder what has happened to us!

MAN'S SOUL—MIND, WILL AND EMOTIONS
. . .

Next, the *soul* consists of a person's mind, will and emotions. In Psalm 42:1-6, David speaks of his soul's passion for God, as well as his soul's decision to hope in God.

The Bible tells us what to do about the soul. Here are a few examples:

> **Keep a cool head. Stay alert. The Devil is poised to pounce, and would like nothing better than to catch you napping. Keep your guard up.**
>
> 1 Peter 5:8 THE MESSAGE

> **And be not conformed to this world: but be ye transformed by the renewing of your mind.**
>
> Romans 12:2

It is our personal responsibility to renew our minds, or our thoughts, with the wisdom of God's Word instead of the wisdom of this world, which is under the power of the evil one. (1 John 5:19.)

Our will is the part of the soul with which we make decisions. We choose to either obey God's Word or to yield to our fears or temptations. Therefore, our will plays a vital role in both making and breaking casualty covenants.

THE BODY—MAN'S "EARTH SUIT"

Finally, man's spirit and soul live inside his *body.* Originally, the Lord God formed the body of the first man, Adam, from the earth.

> **And the Lord God formed man of the dust of the ground, and breathed into his**

nostrils the breath of life; and man became a living soul.

Genesis 2:7

In this life, our bodies are our indispensable "earth suits." Without them, we would be unable to exist on this planet. However, these bodies are susceptible to death.

The last enemy that shall be destroyed is death.

1 Corinthians 15:26

As death came from sin, so our victory over death came from the sacrifice of the Lord Jesus Christ.

Since the children are made of flesh and blood, it's logical that the Savior took on flesh and blood in order to rescue them by his death. By embracing death, taking it into himself, he destroyed the Devil's hold on death and freed all who cower through life, scared to death of death.

Hebrews 2:14,15 THE MESSAGE

Unfortunately, many Christians don't enjoy the benefits of Jesus' victory over physical death. Instead, they open the door to premature death by accepting death wishes—that is, by yielding to the cunning deceptions of the devil. They lose sight of the fact that he is a murderer and the father of lies. And once the devil gets them to agree with his lies, he gains the right to send them to an early grave.

In the Bible, our bodies are sometimes referred to as vessels:

But we have this treasure in earthen vessels, that the excellency of the power may be of God, and not of us.

2 Corinthians 4:7

There is a difference between our present mortal bodies and our future resurrected bodies.

It is sown a natural body; it is raised a spiritual body. There is a natural body, and there is a spiritual body.

1 Corinthians 15:44

But if the Spirit of him that raised up Jesus from the dead dwell in you, he that raised up Christ from the dead shall also quicken your mortal bodies by his Spirit that dwelleth in you.

Romans 8:11

The Good News tells us that we have the very same Holy Spirit within us who raised Christ from the dead. This same Holy Spirit performed all the miracles of Jesus and the disciples, and His gifts of miracles and healings continue today. (1 Cor. 12:28.)

Our Lord Jesus desires divine health for us.

Beloved, I wish above all things that thou mayest prosper and be in health, even as thy soul prospereth.

3 John 1:2

The condition here for prospering is according **as thy soul prospereth.** That means unbelief in God's Word in your *soul,* or your mind, can be a barrier to receiving healing in your *body.*

PLAYING WITH FIRE
. . .

These three elements of spirit, soul and body need to be kept in divine balance, because our enemy is a ruthless opportunist. He seeks to attack us through our bodily senses and our soulish thoughts, will and emotions in order to subvert our communion with God in our spirits.

The devil's strategy is to create a desperate situation in our lives. Then in a moment of crisis, he moves in to strike a bargain—a casualty covenant—with us.

In our vulnerable condition, we often choose the enemy's deceptive solutions instead of God's way of trusting in His mercy and believing in His promises. But God the Father will not interfere with our making wrong choices, because our union with Him is in spirit; He never interferes with our free will.

God established the vital principle of freedom of choice for man, and He does not violate this principle. He does not force His will or way into a life but permits man to make the decision. However, if we choose God's way in obedience to His Word, we have the promise: **If ye be willing and obedient, ye shall eat the good of the land** (Isa. 1:19).

When we covenant with Satan and his demonic host, we unwittingly give him permission to destroy our lives. On the other hand, God has only mercy and goodness in store for us. He tells us:

> **"Come now, let us reason together, says
> the Lord: though your sins are like scarlet,
> they shall be as white as snow; though they**

are red like crimson, they shall become like wool."

Isaiah 1:18 RSV

If we compromise God's truth in His holy Word with Satan's lies from the pit of hell, we have bought into a demonic plan of eventual devastation for ourselves and our loved ones.

It's like making a pet out of a baby boa constrictor. This large snake starts out small. It can be pleasant to play with. Because the boa constrictor is a pet, someone may assume that it is harmless. But it's faulty to think a full-grown boa constrictor is harmless.

That same principle is true for those who flirt with extramarital affairs or dabble in pornography, for example. They are playing with fire!

We may think most everyone plays with fire in some form or another. We may even ask ourselves, *What's wrong with it? After all, everyone is doing it.*

As we begin to make these thought covenants with the enemy, compromising the truth of God's Word, we rarely realize we have signed up for crushing experiences in our lives. But the Bible warns us of exactly that: **And be sure your sin will find you out** (Num. 32:23).

The world system, which Satan largely dominates, often encourages errant behavior that destroys lives, marriages and homes. But despite the fact that "everyone is doing it," the results of such behavior are catastrophic. The marriage covenant, for instance, was instituted by our Creator. (Gen. 2:24; Matt. 19:4-12.) Heartache, disease and guilt often result from breaking that God-ordained covenant if no biblical reasons for divorce exist.

There is pleasure in sin for a season, but "pay-up time" is on the way. (Heb. 11:25.) Eventually, that boa constrictor becomes a full-grown snake, capable of wrapping itself around its owner and crushing him to death!

SATAN'S STRATEGY OF DECEPTION

• • •

Satan lies to the human race. His strategy is to use fear and deception. Liar is his name, and deception is his game.

The Bible tells us that Satan can transform himself into an angel of light. (2 Cor. 11:14.) It describes him as **that old serpent, called the Devil, and Satan, which deceiveth the whole world** (Rev. 12:9).

The Bible also forewarns us:

> **For there shall arise false Christs, and false prophets, and shall shew great signs and wonders; insomuch that, if it were possible, they shall deceive the very elect.**
>
> **Matthew 24:24**

We need to realize that our wily foe has demons that are assigned to become familiar with our lives. These demons are called familiar spirits and are a primary tool in the devil's strategy of deception. (Deut. 18:11,12.) They report to Satan the vulnerable areas in our lives, areas in which we can be duped into essentially agreeing with the devil and thus making a covenant with him. The enemy's goal is that we receive his evil plan for our lives instead of our Creator God's good plan:

For I know the thoughts that I think toward you, saith the Lord, thoughts of peace, and not of evil, to give you an expected end.

Jeremiah 29:11

FIRST AVENUE OF DECEPTION: IGNORANCE
• • •

Let's explore three definite avenues that can open us up to deception. The first avenue is *ignorance of God's holy Word*. Lack of knowledge can cause us to perish: **Where there is no vision, the people perish** (Prov. 29:18). Therefore, God does not excuse ignorance. Instead, He tells us what to do to rid ourselves of it:

This book of the law shall not depart out of thy mouth; but thou shalt meditate therein day and night, that thou mayest observe to do according to all that is written therein: for then thou shalt make thy way prosperous, and then thou shalt have good success.

Joshua 1:8

One way demons inject their suggestions into people's thought life is by leading their minds into a "blank" state—that is, no longer focused on the Word—eventually producing a passive mind that does nothing to overcome ignorance of God's Word. This permits infiltration by the devil's dark forces—always with grave results.

Our Creator God doesn't want us to be passive. He wants us to *cooperate* actively with Him. He created our minds to be used for His glory. That's why the Bible exhorts us: **Do not be vague and thoughtless and foolish, but understanding and firmly grasping what the will of the Lord is** (Eph. 5:17 AMP).

As I heard someone once say, "Common sense is not a foreign coin, so go on and use it!"

Because we do not always recognize the difference between the activity of evil spirits and that of the Holy Spirit or our own human spirits, we can entertain thoughts injected from malevolent spirits without even knowing it.

For instance, we may watch a person cough and sneeze in a flu medication commercial on television and think, *I may be coming down with the same thing! I need to buy that medication.* If we absorb and dwell on that thought of becoming ill, we can actually become sick. The power of suggestion is very real, and that's exactly how you can make a casualty covenant!

The "evil empire"—Satan's kingdom of darkness—is a source of numerous suggestions to the passive mind. Once the victim agrees with satanic suggestions, evil spirits work on that person's environment to fulfill their wicked plans. This is the principle on which fortune-tellers base the fulfillment of their predictions.

The Bible clearly shows that demonic forces can impart ideas:

> **Then Peter took him** [Jesus], **and began to rebuke him, saying, Be it far from thee, Lord: this shall not be unto thee. But he turned, and said unto Peter, Get thee behind me, Satan: thou art an offence unto**

**me: for thou savourest not the things that be
of God, but those that be of men.**

Matthew 16:22,23

Where did Peter get the idea to tell Jesus not to go to Jerusalem and be crucified? We see by Jesus' sharp rebuke that the source of that idea was obviously Satan.

Many people refuse to believe that their minds could receive input from the devil. Their willful ignorance provides a good cover for the evil one to hide behind.

The apostle Paul recognized this danger. In 2 Corinthians 10:4-5 AMP, he warns us to destroy these mental strongholds with the spiritual weapons at our disposal:

For the weapons of our warfare are not physical [weapons of flesh and blood], but they are mighty before God for the overthrow and destruction of strongholds,

[Inasmuch as we] refute arguments and theories and reasonings and every proud and lofty thing that sets itself up against the [true] knowledge of God; and we lead every thought and purpose away captive into the obedience of Christ (the Messiah, the Anointed One).

When a person develops a passive mind, it can be a struggle for him to regain control of his thought life. In order to do so, he can ask God to enlighten him about which lies he has embraced. And once enlightened, he must reject those lies, using the creative power of God's Word. God will help him regain his freedom as he does his part.

In this spiritual battle, the person must exercise his mind and make all of his decisions according to the Word of God.[2] This takes time, but it is vital to his well-being and mental health.

SECOND AVENUE OF DECEPTION: INCORRECT DOCTRINE
• • •

Another avenue that opens us up to deception is *misunderstanding and misapplication of God's truth as set forth in the Bible.* Such doctrinal error could come from church leaders, relatives or others who rationalize or misinterpret certain Scriptures.

For example, you may have been taught to believe that there are no holy angels, unholy angels or demons and that hell does not exist. But Scripture tells us the truth:

But the fearful, and unbelieving, and the abominable, and murderers, and whore-mongers, and sorcerers, and idolaters, and all liars, shall have their part in the lake which burneth with fire and brimstone: which is the second death.

Revelation 21:8

The wicked shall be turned into hell, and all the nations that forget God.

Psalm 9:17

Then shall he say also unto them on the left hand, Depart from me, ye cursed, into everlasting fire, prepared for the devil and his angels.

Matthew 25:41

Or perhaps your denomination teaches that divine healing ended with the apostles and the early church. But God's Word assures us that divine healing is available today. It is a part of the Atonement that Jesus purchased for us with His blood:

Who his own self [Jesus Christ] **bare our sins in his own body on the tree, that we, being dead to sins, should live unto right-eousness: by whose stripes ye were healed.**

1 Peter 2:24

In this Scripture, we clearly see two aspects of the Atonement: 1) Jesus' death on the Cross for our sins and 2) His bodily flesh seared by the whips of the Roman soldiers for our physical benefit. Healing is in the Atonement, and the Atonement is for us today.

The Bible also assures us that **Christ hath redeemed us from the curse of the law, being made a curse for us** (Gal. 3:13). In Deuteronomy 28:61, we find that the curse of the law includes every kind of sickness and disease. But listen to the good news in Deuteronomy 28!

And it shall come to pass, if thou shalt hearken diligently unto the voice of the Lord thy God, to observe and to do all his commandments which I command thee this day, that the Lord thy God will set thee on high above all nations of the earth: and all these blessings shall come on thee, and overtake thee, if thou shalt hearken unto the voice of the Lord thy God.

Deuteronomy 28:1,2

THIRD AVENUE OF DECEPTION: DISOBEDIENCE
• • •

We will enjoy the benefits and blessings of God if we will obey His commandments. On the other hand, disobedience opens us up to curses.

Many believers are ill today because their parents or even grandparents participated in witchcraft and similar practices. But occult curses can be broken in Jesus' name, enabling these people to enjoy the benefit of divine health that is rightfully theirs according to the Word:

Bless the Lord, O my soul, and forget not all his benefits: who forgiveth all thine iniquities; *who healeth all thy diseases.*

Psalm 103:2,3

So we see that the third avenue of deception, disobedience to God's Word—walking contrary to what God tells us to do—also opens the door to casualty covenants. (Deut. 27:15-26.)

In the following chapters, we will discuss further the various ways we may be unintentionally moving contrarily to God's will for our lives. We will also see the amazing benefits that come when we repent and break all wrong covenants, thus putting ourselves in a position to receive from God.

OUR FREEDOM TO CHOOSE
• • •

As you read this chapter, you may be entertaining the thought that Christians could not covenant with Satan's demons or be tempted to enter into agreement with them. But remember, our Creator God has given us free will. He will not violate our God-given right to make our own decisions.

Jesus says, **Behold, I stand at the door, and knock** (Rev. 3:20). We have to invite Him into our hearts by a choice of our will. Though Jesus died for our sins, He does not force Himself or His way of life upon us. We always have the freedom of choice—the liberty to choose His way of abundant life or Satan's way of destruction.

> **I call heaven and earth to record this day against you, that I have set before you life and death, blessing and cursing: therefore choose life, that both thou and thy seed may live.**
>
> **Deuteronomy 30:19**

OUR AUTHORITY OVER CASUALTY COVENANTS
* * *

Sickness or premature death is not always the result of personal sin, but each is always a consequence of the original sin of Adam and Eve. We could say that the entire human race inherited "blood poisoning" from the first two people whom God created. And it came because of their disobedience to God's Word. (Gen. 3:6.) Their sin brought a curse on the ground and caused Satan to acquire their God-given authority.

The crux of the matter is this: God's created man, Adam, *succumbed* to Satan's temptation. God's begotten Son, Jesus Christ, *resisted* Satan's temptation.

> **For we have not an high priest which cannot be touched with the feeling of our**

infirmities; but was in all points tempted like as we are, yet without sin.

Hebrews 4:15

By Jesus' sacrifice on the Cross for the sins of the whole human race and His obedience to His Father's commandments, He regained the authority that Adam had lost.

Today, in the name of Jesus Christ, every believer can exercise that same authority over devils and diseases.

Then he called his twelve disciples together, and gave them power and authority over all devils, and to cure diseases. And he sent them to preach the kingdom of God, and to heal the sick.

Luke 9:1,2

Verily, verily, I say unto you, He that believeth on me, the works that I do shall he do also; and greater works than these shall he do; because I go unto my Father.

John 14:12

Then Peter said, Silver and gold have I none; but such as I have give I thee: in the name of Jesus Christ of Nazareth rise up and walk.

Acts 3:6

Jesus came to planet earth, humbling Himself to be born as a baby from the womb of the virgin Mary. Even though He was God incarnate, He grew up as a man in a body of flesh and blood, suffering and enduring temptation just as we do.

That's why Jesus understands our human weaknesses. He loves and pities His children who worship Him in love. He suffers with us in our sufferings because, in His love, He is one with us.

Jesus bears our griefs and carries our sorrows. (Isa. 53:4.) He never leaves us or forsakes us once we have invited Him into our hearts and our lives. He is faithful. And He has given us the authority in His name to close the doors we may have opened to the enemy through casualty covenants.

THE TEMPTATION

If we are to stay clear of Satan's deceptions, we have to first understand how he goes about tempting us to agree with him. Second, we must learn how we are to respond to his temptations in a way that ultimately puts us in agreement with God.

JESUS' TEMPTATION IN THE WILDERNESS
• • •

Let's consider how Jesus was tempted by the devil after He was baptized in the Jordan River.

Next Jesus was taken into the wild by the Spirit for the Test. The Devil was ready to give it. Jesus prepared for the Test by fasting forty days and forty nights. That left him, of course, in a state of extreme hunger, which the Devil took advantage of in the first test: "Since you are God's Son, speak the word that will turn these stones into loaves of bread."

Jesus answered by quoting Deuteronomy: "It takes more than bread to stay

alive. It takes a steady stream of words from God's mouth."

Matthew 4:1-4 THE MESSAGE

The devil accepted Jesus' divine sonship. He acknowledged Jesus' *ability* to perform a miracle. His purpose, however, was to test Jesus' *motive* in performing a miracle.

Essentially Satan was suggesting that the only thing motivating humanity is the satisfaction of physical appetites; therefore, the devil concluded, materialism and the satisfying of those appetites is mankind's solution. But Jesus' answer to Satan came straight out of God's Word and confirmed that man's spiritual side is much more important.

For the second test the Devil took him to the Holy City. He sat him on top of the Temple and said, "Since you are God's Son, jump." The Devil goaded him by quoting Psalm 91: "He has placed you in the care of angels. They will catch you so that you won't so much as stub your toe on a stone."

Jesus countered with another citation from Deuteronomy: "Don't you dare test the Lord your God."

Matthew 4:5-7 THE MESSAGE

In the second test, we see the satanic device of using isolated Scripture in an attempt to deceive. Jesus didn't fall for that either. He just corrected Satan's using one Scripture out of context by saying, *"Again* it is written..." (v. 7 RSV.)

Jesus showed us here that taking Scriptures out of their context can lead to presumption and fanaticism.

The only way to walk in scriptural authority is to accept the Bible in its entirety. Jesus made it clear to Satan that He wouldn't be so presumptuous as to test God's power to preserve and protect.

> **For the third test, the Devil took him on the peak of a huge mountain. He gestured expansively, pointing out all the earth's kingdoms, how glorious they all were. Then he said, "They're yours—lock, stock, and barrel. Just go down on your knees and worship me, and they're yours."**
>
> **Jesus' refusal was curt, "Beat it, Satan!" He backed his rebuke with a third quotation from Deuteronomy: "Worship the Lord your God, and only him. Serve him with absolute single-heartedness."**
>
> **The Test was over. The Devil left. And in his place, angels! Angels came and took care of Jesus' needs.**
>
> Matthew 4:8-11 THE MESSAGE

Satan understood Jesus' divinely appointed goal. Jesus was the Man born to be the King of kings and Lord of lords. So Satan offered a compromise to Jesus, saying, "Worship me, and I will give you kingship over all the world. You won't have to go the way of the Cross." This compromise would leave Satan in control, because it meant Jesus Christ would reign under the command of Satan, who would then be the ultimate ruler of this world.[1]

The deepest test of a person's heart is whom and what he worships. Jesus Christ passed that test, meeting each of Satan's temptations with God's Word.

We can do the same! We can stay free of evil compromises and covenants!

THE DANGER OF YIELDING TO TEMPTATION

• • •

I want you to notice something amazing about this story. In all of Jesus' temptations in the wilderness, Satan sought to convince the Son of God to *agree* with him. The devil tried to make a covenant with the Lord! Satan offered Jesus the crown without the Cross. Imagine if Jesus had accepted that deceptive offer—the devil would have succeeded in aborting God's plan of redemption!

In the same way, *when we yield to temptation and covenant with the destroyer, we participate in the process of our own destruction.*

That was true in the case of Jesus' disciple Judas. After yielding to the devil's lies, Judas betrayed Jesus for thirty pieces of silver and then went out and hung himself. (Matt. 27:5.) Well, if we buy into the devil's business by agreeing with his lies, in a sense we "hang" ourselves as well. In other words, we give Satan license to work his plan of destruction in our lives.

That's why we must not be ignorant of Satan's devices. His evil empire operates on terror, torture and torment. He has no peace because he is eternally damned and knows it. Even his servants, the demons, know their final outcome is the abyss. (Matt. 8:29-31.) But for now, they want to express their evil nature through the human race in order to achieve their own perverted ends.

So demons try to gain access into our lives, tempting us through lies and deception to sin. We must follow Jesus' example and counter each temptation with God's Word. You see, it's true that there is pleasure in sin for a season—otherwise, we wouldn't be tempted!

Have you ever seen the Bugs Bunny cartoon depicting Elmer using a carrot to bait Bugs into a trap? Sin is sort of like that. Satan uses the same strategy to trick people into making a covenant with him—only he uses the "bait" of illicit pleasure, vainglory, lust and other sins of the flesh to entice them.

But regardless of what form of bait he uses, one thing is for sure—if we take it, we are in danger of becoming trapped within a demonic stronghold, held in bondage until we learn to break free.

We have to stay on guard against the enemy's attempts to lead us down a dark path of deception the same way we guard ourselves in the natural against, say con artists. A con artist finds it convenient to lead his victim into a dark alley to sell him counterfeit goods. He opens his jacket, revealing all sorts of watches hanging on the inside, and then asks, "Want to buy a watch?" However, what seems like a bargain becomes a problem when the con man's assistant hits the person over the head and robs him!

In the same way, meeting with dark forces in dark places of the soul can open the door for spiritual darkness to enter into our lives—especially if we yield to the temptation of agreeing with the biggest con man of all, Satan himself. We cannot let ignorance of God's Word, religious tradition or false teaching cause us to blindly believe that we're too spiritual to be tempted or deceived into making a covenant that results in casualties to ourselves and our loved ones. If Satan tried to tempt Jesus Christ, we can expect him to try to trick us into agreeing with him as well.

A PERSONAL EXPERIENCE WITH CASUALTY COVENANTS
• • •

I was ignorant of this truth when I entered the hospital for routine surgery years ago. Upon waking up from the anesthesia, I was surprised to see my physician standing beside my bed.

She said, "Mrs. Winborn, you have ovarian cancer. Laboratory tests show that it is in the last stages and has metastasized.

"However," she continued, "there is one hope. It's called the gold treatment and involves using a live radioisotope flown in from the nation's stockpile. This chemical element will be inserted within you while it is 'alive,' making you temporarily radioactive.

"Since this is a rather harsh treatment, it will be necessary to give you time between surgeries to recuperate. Provided that you have healed sufficiently to receive this treatment, we will need your permission to do it. Otherwise, Mrs. Winborn, you probably have less than six months to live."

As this grim prognosis sunk in, I began hearing other words in my spirit—the words of Scripture:

There hath no temptation taken you but such as is common to man: but God is faithful, who will not suffer you to be tempted

above that ye are able; but will with the temptation also make a way to escape, that ye may be able to bear it.

1 Corinthians 10:13

I was in physical pain, mentally struggling to sort out all I was hearing. Concluding that the radioisotope was necessary and that my Father God would sustain me through this life-and-death crisis, I agreed to the gold treatment.

I returned home to regain strength before the next surgery. Meanwhile, my family and friends comforted me as they prayed for my full recovery. In fact, entire congregations were united in prayer on my behalf.

About this time, I attended a meeting in the home of my friends Alliene and Wylie Vale of Houston, Texas, where Reverend Kenneth E. Hagin was ministering. Brother Hagin prophesied concerning my condition, saying, "She will be all right." This was an extraordinary word from the Lord, considering the medical prognosis. During that stressful time, I clung to his prophetic words like a person stranded down in a pit, grasping a rope for deliverance.

One night, June Dold, an excellent Bible teacher and friend, invited me to her home. Driving there, I uttered a simple prayer, "Lord, give me a token of Your love."

Another neighbor joined us at June's home, and as the three of us visited together, a wonderful fragrance began to permeate the house. We were puzzled because we could not identify the source of this heavenly perfume. Gradually we became aware that we were experiencing the presence of Jesus.

This is confirmed in Psalm 45:7-8, where the psalmist says of the coming Messiah:

Thou lovest righteousness, and hatest wickedness: therefore God, thy God, hath anointed thee with the oil of gladness above thy fellows. *All thy garments smell of myrrh, and aloes, and cassia,* **out of the ivory palaces, whereby they have made thee glad.**

As we thanked and praised Jesus, the fragrance enveloped us. This experience was an overwhelming token of God's love—a direct answer to my prayers.

When it came time, a skilled physician administered the gold treament. The hospital care was excellent—the best that medical science could offer. All went well, and I was again sent home to recuperate.

Suddenly, a new problem developed. New test results revealed tumors in both of my breasts! Alarmed, I made an appointment with my physician to discuss the test results. My dear friend Alliene, who is a gifted songwriter and Bible teacher, drove me to the doctor's office.

The prognosis wasn't good. The Christian gynecologist had done all she could to help. But after an exam, I gazed into her compassionate eyes and realized my days were limited. Obviously, the cancer had continued to spread.

But I really believed God would heal me. I wanted to live! I had two young sons to raise.

Alliene drove us to my home, where we sat down together on the sofa and were very quiet. I was grateful she did not offer platitudes; her presence was comforting enough.

Unexpectedly, I heard words spoken into my left ear. Apparently the words weren't audible—Alliene didn't hear them—but I heard them clearly. The voice I heard was that of a demonic messenger, who said, *Make a covenant with Satan, and you can live.*

This concept was an utter shock to me! I had never realized before that a Christian could make a covenant with Satan. (Of course, if I had obeyed that voice, I would have made a conscious covenant with the enemy, whereas most people are deceived into making *unconscious* covenants with him.)

This proposition came at a time when it seemed that a dark and final curtain was falling upon my life. I desperately desired to live. Despite so many prayers and all the good care I had received, the ordeal had not ended; instead, it had intensified!

I was not confused about my response to the satanic proposition; it was a deliberate decision. I reasoned, *Satan is certainly real. I know that because I have just heard from him. But if Satan is real, then God is most definitely real! Satan is a liar. Jesus Christ is the truth. I refuse Satan's offer of life. I will trust Jesus Christ, who is life."*

The confrontation was over. I slept soundly that night for the first time in months.

"MIND HEALING" VS. DIVINE HEALING

After that, the Good Shepherd led me to attend a Kathryn Kuhlman miracle service. She had everyone attending the huge meeting pray for me and even personally prayed for my healing. Something left me at that time. I knew it was a spirit of fear. Second Timothy 1:7 really ministered to me at that time.

For God hath not given us the spirit of fear; but of power, and of love, and of a sound mind.

When I returned to Houston after the Kathryn Kuhlman meeting, I still had tumors in my breasts. However, I no longer feared dying. The Holy Spirit kept reminding me of two Scriptures:

I love them that love me; and those that seek me early shall find me.

Proverbs 8:17

It is of the Lord's mercies that we are not consumed, because his compassions fail not. They are new every morning: great is thy faithfulness.

Lamentations 3:22,23

Obeying the Holy Spirit's gentle promptings, I arose early one morning in my home and went into the living room. The house was quiet. The morning was beautiful. The husband and sons I loved so much were still asleep.

Dressed in my gown and robe, I slipped to my knees at the corner of the sofa, bowed my head and said, "Lord, Your Word says You love those who love You and that those who seek You early shall find You. I love You, and I am seeking You early. Your Word also says that Your compassions fail not and Your mercies are new every morning. Lord, I ask You to be merciful to me and let me live to raise the two sons You have given me."

This was the moment of truth. Almost immediately, God began to open my understanding to certain mistakes I'd made. He showed me that, without realizing it, I had counted on my good works to merit special attention from Him.

Right away, I repented of this sin, because God's Word says, **For by grace are ye saved through faith; and that not of yourselves: it is the gift of God: not of works, lest any man should boast** (Eph. 2:8,9).

As I waited quietly before the Lord, He showed me something else: There is a fine line between *divine healing* and *mind healing*. The source of divine healing is Jesus Christ, but mind healing is something else altogether. Mind healing is using the force of your own *will* to make something come to pass through your own stubbornness.

This is the realm of healing I had unconsciously moved into, and the Lord was warning me of its danger:

**For rebellion is as the sin of witchcraft,
and stubbornness is as iniquity and idolatry.**

1 Samuel 15:23

The change from having faith in the finished work of Christ to having faith in my own ability had been so subtle that I was unaware of it when it happened. The Spirit of truth, the Holy Spirit, had to reveal it to me.

HEALED!

I now knew how I had drifted from the simple gospel. I asked God to forgive me. It was easy to say, "Lord, without one plea, I come to Thee,"[2] as the song says. Slowly, an assurance that I was healed began to fill my being until finally my heart was completely and fully assured that *I was healed of cancer!*

Soon after that experience, I had biopsies of the two tumors in my breasts. No cancer was found! Fifteen months later, after much prayer and guidance from the Holy Spirit, I submitted to an exploratory operation by the doctor who had performed the gold treatment. There still wasn't any cancer! I was healed!

And for the sake of backing up my testimony, I continue to have a physical checkup each year, and I always receive a clean bill of health.

The following is an excerpt from a note written by my doctor:

"It has been a privilege and a pleasure to have you for a patient. I have especially appreciated your Christian witness and the simple faith and trust in the Lord which you displayed, even when faced with a very grave prognosis regarding your illness. I am thankful that the Lord has raised you up and has maintained you in good health, free from any recurrence. May you have many more years of fruitful service."

Regarding my case, another doctor said, "That woman certainly experienced a miracle! She had massive malignancy internally. It was nothing but a miracle!"

I am thoroughly convinced that the main reason many people have a recurrence of cancer is their fear that it *will* come back. The evil spirit works on the patient's thought life until he finally capitulates and agrees that cancer will come to him again. By yielding to the fear of cancer, the person essentially agrees, or makes a covenant, with the malevolent spirit behind this disease and becomes the casualty of cancer once again.

Now, I gained the knowledge of casualty covenants through personal experience. I have learned to resist thoughts of fear of a recurrence and have stayed free of cancer for more than thirty years!

RIDDING YOURSELF OF CASUALTY COVENANTS
· · ·

My children are all grown now, and I have grandchildren. Through the years, my own personal experience and the experiences of many others have taught me a great deal about casualty covenants (or, as someone else labeled them, *catastrophic* covenants).

It's so important to realize that Satan wants to keep you in the dark concerning any areas in your soul where you have yielded to the temptation to agree with him. Therefore, it is wise and necessary to pray to the Father God in the name of His Son, Jesus Christ, asking Him to uncover and reveal to you by His Spirit any covenants you may have made with Satan in your life.

Then be ready to receive God's answer and act on it immediately by asking His forgiveness. You can be assured that He will forgive you according to 1 John 1:9:

If we confess our sins, he is faithful and just to forgive us our sins, and to cleanse us from all unrighteousness.

Would you like to break all covenants with Satan you have ever made—consciously, unconsciously or ignorantly? If so, please pray the following prayer:

Father God, in Your Son's name, Jesus Christ, I ask You to forgive me of all my sins and for making any covenants with Satan. I

**break those covenants in the name of Jesus!
I am now completely free from them. They
have no control or power over me from this
moment on! Jesus came to set me free, and
I am free indeed! Amen.**

Hallelujah! And now that you've been set free from
casualty covenants in your life, I want to bring to light
some specific ways in which Satan works to tempt you to
agree with his lies. You see, only by knowing his destructive strategies can you avoid and overcome them. I
believe that with the light of God's truth, you can live
victoriously, free from casualty covenants!

4

EMOTIONAL BONDAGE

The enemy has many plans of attack against us. One of these is emotional bondage. Damaged emotions can open our souls to accepting the deceptive "solution" of a casualty covenant. When we are wounded and hurting, the enemy of our souls torments us and tempts us to blame God. But the truth is, the devil is usually at the root of the very problem to which he offers solution. That's why we must run *to* our Father God and never *from* Him.

RUN TO GOD

Now, we can blame God for our bad experiences, or we can run to Him with our troubles. He knows that we are made of dust; and as a father pities his children, so the Lord pities those who fear Him. (Ps. 103:13,14.)

For instance, when Adam and Eve hid from their Creator in the Garden because of their disobedience to Him, His love was still there for them. Though they had brought trouble upon themselves and the entire human race, God had mercy on Adam and Eve and did not destroy them.

Our emotions can rebel and rage against God when we experience unanswered prayers or other distresses, but this is the very time we should turn to Him with our damaged emotions, because **God is our refuge and strength, a very present help in trouble** (Ps. 46:1).

Satan has other weapons too. Shyness, loneliness and fear of rejection are insecurities that enable the enemy to work in our thought life. Like the thief he is, he comes to our thoughts to persuade us to isolate ourselves from others. Satan seeks to convince us that to be safe from wounds, we must build walls around ourselves to keep others out. The problem is that the walls we build to keep others out also keep us *in!*[1]

When we choose to erect invisible walls with the brick and mortar of damaged emotions, we immediately stop all spiritual growth. We become sitting ducks for the devil, and suddenly he can hit us with all kinds of misunderstanding and poor judgment. We can become so befuddled that we make it easy for the enemy to enter into our decision-making processes and misguide us. That's when his demons are able to deal death blows to our self-esteem and our relationships with others.

I like what the late Dr. Lester Sumrall said: "If you're moping, you aren't coping!"[2]

The following are examples of casualty covenants made from emotional hang-ups that affect all of us in different ways as we make life choices for good or for evil.

REJECTION

Sometimes emotional and mental "structures" have existed for years, and we may need to wage a real mental war in order to tear them down. We may not even remember when those evil structures were built.

For example, it is possible for a spirit of rejection to enter a mother's womb and affect the newborn baby. No matter how much loving care the child receives, the evil spirit of rejection will tell him that he is unloved, worthless and stupid, robbing him of his self-esteem.

As that child enters into adulthood, he will become emotionally crippled, unaware that many of his actions and decisions are based on his old feelings of rejection. This maladjustment could cause him to sabotage his own life by making faulty decisions based on feelings of rejection.

When we accept a thought pattern of rejection, we program ourselves for rejection. I witnessed this behavior pattern in a lovely Christian lady. She desired to meet a compatible Christian man. So, after mutual prayer, another friend and I decided to bring her and an old friend of mine together at a dinner party.

This woman was cultured, intelligent, attractive and divorced. The man was handsome, witty, intelligent and divorced. But at the dinner party, she completely ignored him, spending all her time conversing with another guest. The man concluded that the woman was a snob, and he would not pursue the relationship.

People who appear snobbish are often really just shy. Shyness can be a form of fear, making the person a victim instead of a victor in life.

What happened? The lady had experienced rejection in the past from her father and ex-husband. Ever since childhood, she had been programmed for rejection. At the dinner party she was not rejected; however, she set herself up for rejection by totally ignoring the Christian man.

Afterwards, she slowly realized her actions had brought about the very thing she feared—*rejection!* In fact, the fear of rejection had such a stronghold on her that she would tremble whenever she became attracted to a man.

In Charles Solomon's book *The Ins and Out of Rejection*, he compares a person pursuing love to a dog chasing a car:

> If he ever caught it, he wouldn't know what to do with it! When a person has never had love, he doesn't know what to do with it when he gets it. Therefore he finds some way to get the loving person to reject him so he will exhibit a behavior or emotion with which he can cope. Then, he blames the rejection on the other person and everything is back to status quo.[3]

As we prayed again over the young woman's relationship with the man whom she'd met at the dinner party, we asked the Lord to reweave the pattern of these two Christians' lives together. Fortunately, the pattern the Lord rewove was stronger than the woman's pattern of rejection. These two people became close companions for the next couple of years and have remained loyal friends.

Joyce Meyer makes an important point about this type of situation in her book *The Root of Rejection:*

> If you have a root of rejection or are in the unfinished process of being healed from rejection, there is the probability that what you perceive as more rejection is really not rejection at all. You may be going through unnecessary torment—torment that will dissipate if you can just learn that those feelings you have are coming from that old root and those old ways of believing.[4]

The Christian woman at the dinner party had made a covenant with a spirit of rejection to *stay* rejected. Oftentimes, this spirit will set a person up to be attracted to someone who cannot or will not return his or her feelings.

For instance, a spirit of rejection may entice you to yearn after a married person or someone who is already committed to another. If you yield to that yearning, you have just helped set up the process for rejection.

The Bible warns, **Thou shalt not covet thy neighbour's house, thou shalt not covet thy neighbour's wife...nor any thing that is thy neighbour's** (Ex. 20:17). It also says that covetousness is actually idolatry. (Col. 3:5.)

In his book *Overcoming Rejection*, Frank Hammond states:

> Rejection causes a wound to "self." When self is wounded, many abnormalities can, and usually do, develop within one's personality.
>
> The wounded personality is prone to become peculiar and unstable in behavior, attitudes and opinions. Also, physical infirmities often emerge out of the emotional stress of one's rejection.
>
> ...Love defeats the devil, but rejection opens a door of opportunity for the devil to do an evil work. Satan builds his kingdom upon rejection.[5]

We can attempt to minister to these self-inflicted wounds of rejection by overindulging in television, alcohol, drugs, sex, business, food, material things, sports and so forth. These can also become idols in our lives. However, "what first appears as liberation is later discovered to be bondage."[6]

When we turn to these things instead of turning to God, they become idols. Idolatry is a sin simply because it takes first place in our lives. That is why God says, **Thou shalt have no other gods before me** (Ex. 20:3).

The root of rejection has many branches: loneliness, fantasy and self-pity, for example. After a person feels rejected, Satan manipulates these "branches of rejection" in the victim's life so the person will make unconscious agreements with him.

FANTASY

The following is a testimony of a young girl whom the devil conned into making a covenant with fantasy—another tool the devil uses to manipulate our emotions.

My parents divorced when I was seven years old. Soon after the divorce, my mother decided to move to another state, taking my older brother and me with her. We moved to a beautiful resort island. A few months later, my dad called and asked for my brother to move back home and live with him.

I remember feeling so heartbroken because my only brother would soon have to leave me. My mother, probably struggling with her own sorrow, told me that I was being "too sensitive." So she unselfishly agreed to let my older brother live with my dad. Meanwhile, I would stay with her.

For the most part, I grew up feeling very lonely and rejected. I so desperately wanted friends but was too shy to make any. For the next sixteen years, I repressed all my emotions, hiding them so that no one would ever know how I felt. My heart was a secret, and as I believe the Lord later showed me, so was my life.

When I was a senior in high school, the Lord revealed an undetected sin in my life: I was living inside a fantasy world. Because I had been lonely for so many years, I had created a happy world inside my mind where I could be safe from rejection. I would pretend I had friends and boyfriends with me wherever I went. I was constantly entertaining fantasies—just about every minute of the day.

I knew the Lord was showing me that my desire for friends was so strong that it had become an idol in my heart. Then He directed me to Matthew 6:33: **Seek ye first the kingdom of God, and his righteousness; and all these things shall be added unto you.**

By the grace of God, I released that demanding desire in my heart. Later I attended a wonderful, renowned Christian college, and the Lord blessed me with better friends than I could have ever chosen for myself. But I wrestled with that fantasy spirit off and on for the next several years.

I knew God was dealing with me. In His divine providence, one day I turned on the radio and heard a Christian man teaching on the danger of fantasizing! He said that when we concoct fantasies for our lives, God cannot meet us where we are, because we have a very *real* God, and fantasy is definitely not real.

Then a dear Christian friend told me about a vision that the Lord had given him of me. In the vision, he saw me playing in a *dark playground,* but the Lord came and rescued me out of it.

That made sense to me, because 1 John 1:5-6 says, **God is light, and in him is no darkness at all. If we say that we have fellowship with him, and walk in darkness, we lie, and do not the truth.** And I also knew that God's Word instructs us to meditate on whatever is true and honest. (Phil. 4:8.)

Fantasy and vain imaginations are not true or honest. In essence, being caught up in fantasy is living a lie. It's like secretly playing with an evil spirit who steals our time and fills our imagination with false reality. Instead, we are to spend our time **casting down imaginations, and every high thing that exalteth itself against the knowledge of God, and bringing into captivity every thought to the obedience of Christ** (2 Cor. 10:5).

I always felt so condemned when I let myself escape into my fantasy world. I knew God wanted me free from this bondage, but I couldn't seem to let it go, even though I had more friends than I had ever dreamed of having. It wasn't until the roots of rejection and loneliness were exposed that I was able to walk in freedom from the bondage of fantasy that had kept me ensnared for so many years.

Finally, God in His mercy revealed to me how I had been duped into unconsciously agreeing with this fantasy spirit that it would protect me from ever being left alone again. I sensed God was telling me that I had a security issue to deal with.

The Lord then compassionately explained to me that whenever you have a void in your heart, something must fill it. He gave me a simple illustration in a vision of water being poured into an ice cube tray; the water always filled the holes first.

I came to understand that when my brother had left me, Satan had sent the spirit of fantasy to fill that void. I had thought the fantasies protected me from being alone. But what a deception that was!

That evil spirit never protected me. Those fantasies did nothing but envelop me in a fake world. No wonder I spent so many years lonely and rejected—I wasn't connecting with reality at all.

Later, the Lord showed me that I had spent the past several years trying to get rid of this fantasy spirit in my own strength, but of course, I failed. This revelation caused me to think that I had also failed to please God. But He reassured me that even if I gave up fantasy, I wouldn't be any more "righteous" in His sight, because Jesus had already made me righteous by His blood when I first became a child of God.

For he hath made him to be sin for us, who knew no sin; that we might be made the righteousness of God in him.

2 Corinthians 5:21

I knew that the Bible says it is impossible to please God without faith. (Heb. 11:6.) So from then on, I agreed to have faith in God and to trust that Jesus' death truly freed me from sin and bondage.

For sin shall not have dominion over you: for ye are not under the law, but under grace.... Being then made free from sin, ye became the servants of righteousness.

Romans 6:14,18

As Paul said, where great sin abounds, a much greater grace is found! (Rom. 5:20.)

SELF-PITY

• • •

Another emotional hang-up the devil uses to get us to make casualty covenants is self-pity.

Tears in our souls can bring tears to our eyes. Who hasn't been wounded by deception in others? The danger, though, is in wallowing in self-pity from the memory of those wounds. As a poet has put it, "*We waste half our strength in a useless regretting,/We sit by old tombs in the dark too long.*"[7]

When thoughts of self-pity attack us, we often throw a "pity party," inviting spectators of past hurts to contribute their sad stories. As we agree with these negative thoughts, we are prone to make covenants with spirits of jealousy, resentment, unforgiveness and self-pity. This compounds the suffering and brings infection to our inner wounds.

Our only avenue of freedom is to first understand that *forgiving all others, including ourselves, is a prerequisite for receiving healing of inner hurts.*

A pity party may temporarily attract a few sympathizers, but ultimately it chases them away. Everyone has his or her own problems. There is enough trouble for everyone in this world! We are no fun to be around when we are wallowing in self-pity.

> Self-pity is more than a familiar mood; it is a harmful mood. Few attitudes toward life are more debilitating. Self-pity saps morale and weakens courage. It eats away the personality like some strong acid. It makes one resentful, jealous, frustrated, gloomy.[8]

God knows that most of us have engaged at one time or another in self-pity. Certainly we have all been mistreated, used and abused at some time. But extended thoughts of self-pity can be a killer because they often lead to depression, despair and suicide.

The bittersweet poison of self-pity lets us think on *self.* We get to be center stage, seeking attention and sympathy for the duration of our pity parties. However, if we spend too much time on this act of futility, we don't get any better. In fact, we actually get worse because we are giving over our energy and time to hurt feelings and damaged emotions.

For years, I sought to help a particular person with a problem she had, marveling all the while at how upset she became over minor annoyances. I struggled to stay patient and compassionate. This person needed loving help.

After years of trying to help, I began to pray for God's knowledge of her true problem. One day in the midst of teaching my Bible class, I had a quick, revealing vision of this woman's true spiritual state.

In the vision stood a giant who looked like a strong pirate. The pirate giant was very much in control. On one of his extended arms sat my friend in swaddling clothes. She looked to be about six months old.

In a flash of revelation, I knew the name of the giant: It was self-pity. My friend's life was dominated by a spirit of self-pity. It had stunted her spiritual growth, leaving her dependent, immature and helpless.

My sympathy had done her no good. Listening to her complaints had worn me down. Informing her about her problem of self-pity didn't work either. Pride caused her to deny its existence in her life.

These types of blind spots are very costly. Proverbs 23:7 says, **For as he thinketh in his heart, so is he.** If we maintain the cause of our distress, we will eventually reap the results.

The truth is, Jesus Christ wanted to set this woman free. By denying that the problem existed, she denied herself His power of deliverance from self-pity and its entanglements. She did not break her covenant with self-pity—*but you can break yours!*

Compassion is needful, but sympathy often courts a whiner. Sympathy originates more from mental emotions, whereas compassion comes from the heart and spirit. Compassion strengthens; sympathy often weakens.

Once we have fallen into the pit of self-pity, how can we free ourselves from this debilitating *"dis*ease"? If we have made a covenant with an evil spirit of self-pity, we may need others to pray with us to escape this entrapment as we verbally break the covenant in the power of the name of Jesus Christ.

We must confess the sin of self-centeredness and pride. Then we must ask for special grace from our Lord Jesus Christ to pull down the stronghold of wrong thoughts engineered by the enemy of our souls.

This pattern of self-destructive thoughts doesn't form overnight, so it may take awhile to break the habit of self-pity. But in Christ, we can do all things! (Phil. 4:13.)

Some say that self-pity is the root of depression. As we seek to overcome self-pity, we should edify ourselves with stories of others who have overcome great adversity. Sometimes we may even need medication and rest in order to recuperate. Another way to overcome self-pity is by serving others.

However, the greatest help is to first break our agreement with a spirit of self-pity in Jesus' name. Then we must determine to obey God by meditating on **things true, noble...the best, not the worst; the beautiful, not the ugly; things to praise, not things to curse** (Phil. 4:8 THE MESSAGE).

Changing our thought patterns is difficult, but it can be done when we line up our minds with God's powerful Word. He formed the world with His Word—that's how powerful it is!

That same creative Word also tells us how to be set free from emotional bondage. We must turn *to* God instead of *away from* Him—trusting Him for our answers instead of blaming Him for our problems. Then, even in the midst of life's trials, we can put on the garment of praise for the spirit of heaviness! (Isa. 61:3.)

5

MENTAL BONDAGE

Many of the casualty covenants people make threaten their relationships with others. The source of these wrong covenants is often a controlling spirit and its counterpart, a spirit of codependency. Satan uses these to attack us with mental bondage.

BEWARE OF CONTROLLING SPIRITS

· · ·

A person operating under a controlling spirit may consistently condemn another person's perceived mistakes. The controller often repeatedly tells the codependent person that he or she is stupid and worthless. This mental battering eventually causes the codependent one to receive and accept these lies as truth, thereby agreeing with the accuser that he or she is inferior and of no value.

In his book *Breaking Controlling Powers,* Roberts Liardon explains why this dynamic is so prevalent in relationships: "Controllers try to act like God, because controlling spirits make people serve their needs and wants."[2]

A good friend of mine shared an apt analogy about this:

> Unfortunately, a controller can ensnare a victim in the same way that a spider can ensnare a dragonfly. Just as the dragonfly gets caught in the web as it tries to get closer to the light, a dependent can become entangled by the controller and prevented from getting closer to God, the light of truth.
>
> Both the dragonfly and the victim are helpless. While the spider eats first the head, then the heart and lastly the body, the controller destroys first the mind, then the soul and lastly the body of the dependent. A controlling spirit uses, abuses and discards. The Holy Spirit loves, cherishes and honors.

Isaiah 59:5-6 says,

They hatch cockatrice eggs and weave the spider's web: he that eateth of their eggs, dieth, and that which is crushed breaketh out into a viper. Their webs shall not become garments, neither shall they cover themselves with their works: their works are works of iniquity, and the act of violence is in their hands.

Many men and women are guilty of the sin of controlling others. In fact, control is what causes many to become spiritual castaways. *Therefore, beware of control as you seek to go deeper into God's truth.*

A controlling spirit has more tentacles than an octopus. When this evil spirit resides in a person, other people who interact with the controller may encounter an entire company of subsidiary evil spirits as well.

For example, people with a controlling type of personality are prone to make covenants with pride, deceit, fear, jealousy, competition, condemnation, intimidation, accusation, manipulation, selfishness and criticism. A desire for attention and a tendency to send others on guilt trips also seem to be a part of this nest of vipers.

No wonder a person with a controlling spirit is sometimes accused of practicing witchcraft! Witches knowingly use evil spirits to accomplish their devious purposes. Similarly, a controller often yields to evil spirits as he manipulates others to serve his selfish ends.

Roberts Liardon writes,

> Another variation of spiritual manipulation is controlling prayers. They're a mild form of witchcraft! ...What is witchcraft? It's the attitude, "You live or die because I say so." It's curses. What are curses? Words spoken against you on behalf of someone else's desires.[3]

A controlling spirit often throws out a dark net of evil spirits to encircle the victim, bringing that person into subjection. This satanic snare can squeeze the very life and hope out of those who come under its influence.

People with controlling spirits are usually stubborn and steeped in what I call *will worship*—magnifying their own wills above all else. Their exaltation of self causes them to assume the place of God in other people's lives. They are also extremely limited in their capacity to show love to others because of their severe selfishness.

Revelation 22:15 refers to the person engaged in this work of the carnal nature as a *sorcerer.* Yet Christians who operate under the influence of controlling spirits are often totally blind to their sin.

Again, Roberts Liardon shares,

> When the controller moves outside the realm of his authority and seeks to control others against their will, he

can be operating in soulish or physic power. Therefore, principles of witchcraft can unknowingly be used by the controller to cause others to submit to him.[4]

King Ahab is a good example of someone who was dominated by a controller. His wife, Jezebel, had an extremely dominating, controlling spirit. In fact, she was a real she-devil!

The "Jezebel spirit" that operated through Ahab's wife is still very much in operation on the earth. It secretly studies the personality of each individual and then chooses the best "bait" to use to seduce him or her into its control.

Of this, *The King James* says, **Notwithstanding I have a few things against thee, because thou sufferest that woman Jezebel, which calleth herself a prophetess, to teach and to seduce my servants** (Rev. 2:20).

For example, if a person is magnanimous, the evil spirits will permit him to perform some charitable acts, thereby creating the idea in the person's mind that he is a giver. Spirits of darkness then try to use these actions of giving and serving to convince the person that he is not a controller, since controllers are usually takers. This strategy often keeps the Christian in darkness, preventing him from repenting and receiving deliverance from the evil forces of witchcraft that are secretly working through his life.

Satan seeks to mask his covert activities of control and manipulation, so it's up to us to get wise and kick him out of our lives!

CONTROLLERS VS. CODEPENDENTS
• • •

Once we recognize the complexity of human nature, it should be a simple thing to agree with the famous old saying by Edward Wallis Hoch:

> There is so much good in the worst of us,
> And so much bad in the best of us,
> That it hardly becomes any of us
> To talk about the rest of us.[5]

As Christians, our orders from "heavenly headquarters" are to love one another and treat others as we want to be treated. However, many Christians do not fulfill these divine commandments in their relationships with others. They are deceived by the enemy into becoming either controllers or codependents—both of which are equally destructive to their spiritual walk.

In today's book market, we often read about the codependent personality. However, there isn't much information available regarding the controller.

Simply stated, the controlling personality is looking for someone to *control*, whereas the codependent is looking for someone to *depend on*. Most everyone encounters these two types of personalities at one time or another.

CHARACTERISTICS OF THE CONTROLLER
• • •

Let's look at some of the prominent characteristics of a controlling personality.

A protective shield that controllers often use is the belief that they are always right. Using this lie as their premise, they typically become abusive and angry with any who question their dictatorship.

Therefore, the codependent, fearing the controller's rejection, often fails to pursue truth. Instead, he settles for living in the shadows of the controller's darkness.

A prayer leader and co-founder of Joysprings, Barbara James describes the situation this way:

> A deep-seated energy of fear usually rules the controller, causing such an individual to build false protective shields in a self-attempt for fleshly defense. They often use control of money, either lavishly given or greedily withheld, to manipulate the one being controlled. In this process, they are actually establishing a spiritual seat of power in their hearts that prohibits life and fortifies darkness. The tyranny of fear and cloak of deception create powerful blocks to the release that is needed.
>
> The dependent also must pray that God will tear down every false shield and build up the shield of truth in the inner man. It is often difficult for the shield of truth to be established because the person has a problem standing fast in God's truth. Most of the time, this creates a great struggle because of the inner conflict and emotional turmoil the dependent is experiencing. There may be a legitimate desire for truth, but the pain of coming to that truth often delays the process of deliverance, healing and freedom.

Controllers are convinced they are right. When confronted with their devious sins of lying, manipulation, accusation, condemnation and competitiveness, they react with denial. Furthermore, controllers often wage counterattacks. They accuse their victims of the very sins they themselves have committed!

This "leapfrog" reaction overwhelms codependents almost every time, sending them on guilt trips and plunging them into such self-recrimination that they may question their own mental stability. This in turn puts stress on the shaky structure of the codependent's self-esteem.

Those who seek to control most often violate others' freedom in order to accommodate their own self-centeredness. However, they assume the role of victim when they desire personal attention and sympathy. The spirit of self-pity keeps them from maturing and seeing themselves or others realistically. As violators, they not only deceive themselves, but they catch others in their webs of deception.

The controller practices many strategies on the codependent's personality structure in his attempt to bring it down to the ground. He can be charming or spiteful. But either way, control is the name, and power is the game—and the ultimate victory is the conquest of the codependent's life.

That's why controllers and codependents who become romantically involved are so often destined for shattered relationships. Such relationships can lead to marriages made in hell, often resulting in battered wives, abused husbands, alcoholics and the like.

Christians with controlling attitudes are often attracted to a legalistic lifestyle based on isolated Old Testament Scriptures that leave out God's love and grace. The Christian who wants to control relies more on man-made rules and formulas than on God's Word. This can result in self-righteousness and rigid adherence to rules similar to the Pharisees' of Jesus' day.

A Pharisee's performance may look great to the outsider, but on the inside he is full of "dead men's bones." (Matt. 23:27.) Those dead bones could represent the people whom Pharisaic controllers have destroyed through their abuse.

Controllers are often gifted with good administrative and leadership abilities. However, they misuse their natural leadership gifts by viewing others as their servants. Also, because controllers recognize the liberty that results when people experience joy, they generally do not encourage joyous attitudes among those they control.

It is very hard for controlling people to give up their drive to dominate and control. They become blinded to their situation and hooked on the personal gratification of their selfish egos. Their self-centeredness also prevents them from viewing other people correctly.

A helpful hymn for a controller to meditate on is "Have Thine Own Way, Lord"[6] because rarely is such a person willing to honestly yield to the Holy Spirit. It is a challenge he doesn't want to contemplate.

Since controlling others is likened to witchcraft, those who are guilty of this sin are in serious spiritual trouble. Fortunately, nothing is too hard for God. (Gen. 18:14.) He can free controlling people as soon as they are ready to cooperate with Him. All they have to do is repent and follow Him into the liberty of humility and obedience.

THE CHARACTERISTICS OF CODEPENDENTS

Codependents need a deep understanding of God's love for them and His unconditional acceptance of them. Otherwise, their own weaknesses easily entangle them, causing them to make covenants with self-pity, martyrdom, condemnation, resentment, bitterness and hatred. Without that deep revelation of God's love for them, they may also yield to depression, despair and suicidal thoughts or experience debilitating, stress-related illnesses.

Codependancy is an emotional condition developed over time by an individual as a behavioral pattern that is self-defeating. This learned behavior results from his sense of low self-worth. This form of coping with life and others is unhealthy.

Codependents, whether Christian or not, are usually very responsible people who make faithful employees. However, they have a tendency to become overly concerned with others, spending too much time minding other people's business.

Christians with a codependency problem are often attracted to the New Testament concept of doing good works and being benevolent and loving toward others. The "royal" commandment in James 2:8, **Thou shalt love thy neighbour as thyself,** is especially meaningful to codependent Christians. However, they tend to ignore the words *as thyself* in that Scripture. Their low self-esteem prevents them from loving themselves adequately.

Codependents desperately need affirmation and love. Accordingly, they often try too hard to please other people and run the risk of idolizing others. Because God forbids idolatry, these people are also in serious spiritual trouble. Yet most codependents don't even recognize the unhealthy feelings and desires that perpetuate their problem.

Melody Beattie, in her book *The Language of Letting Go,* explains another problem that codependents experience:

> Whenever we begin to experience the fullness and joy
> of life, we may feel guilty about those we've left behind—
> those not recovering, those still in pain. This survivor guilt is
> a symptom of codependency.[7]

After putting others first for so long, codependents may lose a sense of their own individuality. So they may feel overwhelmed when they learn that they are part of their own problem, and the thought of making drastic changes in their reactions to the controlling demands of others may seem like a dreaded step into a fearful unknown.

Fortunately, nothing is impossible with God. (Luke 1:37.) When codependents repent and give up fear, truly trusting in Almighty God, He is then able to lead them into freedom. A helpful hymn for them to sing and meditate on as they learn to live free from control is "Great Is Thy Faithfulness."[8]

These controlling and codependent fractures in people's personality structures reside in the realm of the soul. As people come to know and obey God's Word, they can overcome these types of soulish strongholds and mental bondage with the help of the Holy Spirit through prayer. As the Scripture says, God is looking for these very people to worship Him in spirit and in truth. (John 4:23.)

HYPNOTIC CONTROL
• • •

Hypnosis is a door that opens some people to a spirit of control. In their book *Hypnosis and the Christian*, Martin and Diedre Bobgan present a thoughtful appraisal of this controversial subject.

Martin and Diedre explain that hypnotism

> ...does violate the will. The normal evaluating abilities
> are submerged, and choice is made according to suggestion
> without the balance of rational restraint.... Because of this,
> we add the possibility of will violation to the list of reasons
> why Christians should be wary of hypnosis.[9]

In their book, Martin and Diedre Bobgan quote Professor of Psychiatry Thomas Szasz as describing hypnosis as the therapy of a "fake science."[10] We cannot call hypnosis a science, but we can say that it has been an integral part of the occult for thousands of years. The Bible verifies this:

> **There shall not be found among you any one that maketh his son or his daughter to pass through the fire, or that useth divination, or an observer of times, or an enchanter [hypnotist], or a witch. Or a charmer, or a consulter with familiar spirits, or a wizard, or a necromancer. For all that do these things are an abomination unto the Lord: and because of these abominations the Lord thy God doth drive them out from before thee.**
>
> **Deuteronomy 18:10-12**
>
> **Regard not them that have familiar spirits, neither seek after wizards, to be defiled by them: I am the Lord your God.**
>
> **Leviticus 19:31**

Through the years as I've ministered in many nations around the world, I have discovered that a person's involvement in any occult activity can bring a curse on him and his descendants, resulting in all kinds of diseases and misfortunes.

Hypnotism is dangerous because any practice that develops a passive mental state can open one up to forces of darkness.

If you or your family have been involved in any form of the occult, you may have a curse on your life. Now, as a Christian, you can immediately break all curses over yourself in the name of your Lord Jesus Christ, who hung on a tree and became a curse for you. (Gal. 3:13.)

I have known two people who had hypnotic spirits operating through their voices in conversation. One was a man, a radio announcer, who was romantically involved with a friend of mine. He seemed to have some kind of influence over her. I spent some time with the two of them and perceived that a hypnotic influence originated in his voice. I realized that somehow I had to break the control this young man had over my friend, who did not want to see him anymore.

I don't believe the man knew a hypnotic spirit was operating through him. I didn't tell him. But I did try to divert this man's conversational hold on my friend. This agitated him. He may not have known about hypnosis, but he knew from experience that he controlled people by his voice, and he wanted to maintain that control. Eventually, my friend escaped the young man's possessiveness, and he moved away.

The other person with this spirit in operation was a woman who had a lovely outward appearance but who also had one huge fault: She talked constantly! It was a long time before I understood that by her excessive talking, this woman controlled people through the manifestation of a hypnotic spirit.

Now, just because a person is talkative doesn't necessarily mean a hypnotic spirit is present. Some people have a tendency to talk a lot out of habit or nervousness. They can also be talkative in order to build walls around themselves to keep others from knowing them intimately. Sometimes they just love the sound of their own voice. However, hypnotic spirits *can* work through people's voices to control others, so stay alert!

Protect yourself from hypnosis. For that matter, be on guard against anyone who wants to control and dominate you. God has given you a free will to choose, and He doesn't want you to allow casualty covenants with controlling spirits to drain the life out of you and keep you in mental bondage. That's why in 2 Corinthians 3:17, God gives you a spiritual barometer to help you determine what is and what is not of Him: **Where the Spirit of the Lord is, there is *liberty*.**

6

CASUALTY COVENANTS
AND YOUR HEALTH

Physicians know that our emotions can cause physical problems in our bodies. For instance, the emotion of fear can cause heart attacks. And anxiety, which is a form of fear, can not only make us sick but also prevent us from receiving God's divine gift of healing.

Also, prolonged stress can produce an elevated adrenaline level, thus damaging the arteries and heart. In his book *Adrenaline and Stress,* Dr. Archibald D. Hart states,

> Recent research suggests that one way excessive stress causes illness is by destroying the body's immunological defense mechanisms. In other words, too much stress saps the body's ability to fight off disease, so that viruses and bacteria thrive.[1]

Distress can come from real problems in our lives that seem impossible to solve in the natural. But we have an Almighty God who is *supernatural.* He can handle any situation we face! After all, He managed to create the world without our input. You may recall the pointed question He asked Job: **Where were you when I laid the foundation of the earth?** (Job 38:4 AMP).

GOD'S PATHWAY OF HEALING
• • •

Our Good News, the gospel, tells us that God provided divine healing for the sick.

Now, some sincere Christians believe that miracles and supernatural healing, as described in the Scriptures, are not for today. They believe that these manifestations of God's power ceased to operate on the earth when the last apostle died.

This doctrinal stance puts me in a rather awkward position, having received a miracle from the Holy Spirit of the living God! As I have shared, my miraculous healing of terminal ovarian cancer has been confirmed by the two physicians who attended me.

Remember, I was given approximately six months to live, and despite all the excellent medical care I received and all the concerned prayers that were prayed on my behalf, I faced the prospect of imminent death.

This siege of sickness went on for more than two years. Throughout the ordeal, I learned to respect and love those in the medical profession, the majority of whom are made up of dedicated people. I also learned that God heals in different ways. He may use physicians. He may use surgery. He may use medication. He may use special diets. He may use special treatments. And He may use a combination of natural elements, such as vitamins, minerals and so forth.

I once heard a pastor in Houston say, "When I have a headache, I anoint an aspirin and take it!"

I think Dr. Reginald Cherry of Houston, Texas, said it best. He coined the phrase "God's pathway of healing."[2]

The important thing for each person to do is to find God's pathway of healing for his or her particular situation.

HEALING IS STILL FOR TODAY

• • •

The Bible abounds with stories of healings and miracles. Jesus Christ hasn't changed. *His Holy Spirit flowing through believers today still brings forth gifts of healings and miracles—even creative miracles!* (Mark 16:17,18.)

As I minister to people around the world, I continually see miracles occur right before my eyes. I know from the Word and from personal experience that God wants to heal people. He wants to make them whole in their spirits, souls and bodies.

Actually, divine healing occurs first in our human spirits and then is manifested in our bodies. God is a Spirit. Therefore, He heals us through our spirits. His healing does not come through the mind, as some occult religions claim.

I believe Jesus uses healing miracles to open the hearts of unbelievers so they may know Him. More than that, I know that God is merciful and heals many just because of His love and mercy. Psalm 25:10 AMP says, **All the paths of the Lord are mercy and steadfast love, even truth and faithfulness are they for those who keep His covenant and His testimonies.**

God healed me in His mercy. However, do I see everyone healed when I pray for them? *No.*

We have explored some reasons why needy individuals do not receive a healing miracle. Casualty covenants

97

have been the devil's hidden, secret device to deceive many into remaining sick or dying prematurely. Inheritance curses can also be a factor in a person's inability to receive a miracle from God. (We will discuss curses in more depth later.)

As I mentioned earlier, all believers possess the ability to break any casualty covenant or curse that has adversely affected their lives. They do this by exercising their authority over the devil's strategies in the name of Jesus Christ, the divine Son of God.

TWO SIDES OF THE ATONEMENT

We have already seen that Jesus' sufferings apply to both spiritual and physical healing. We can read about these two aspects of the Atonement in Isaiah 53, 1 Peter 2:24 and Matthew 8:17.

Also, we saw in Galatians 3:13 that Jesus Christ redeemed us from the curse of the law when He was made a curse for us. We are redeemed not only from the curses of spiritual death and poverty, but from the curses of sickness and disease!

You see, we may not choose to believe that God has provided healing for us as part of His redemptive plan. But regardless of what we personally believe, *the Word of God is still the truth!*

In Matthew 15:22-28, we read of the Canaanite woman crying out to Jesus to heal her daughter. At first, Jesus explained to her that He was sent only to the lost sheep of the house of Israel. (Notice in verse 26 that Jesus refers to healing as *the children's bread.*) However, the woman persisted, entreating Him to help her.

Then Jesus answered her, O woman, great is your faith! Be it done for you as you wish. And her daughter was cured from that moment.

Matthew 15:28 AMP

There are many reasons why people are not healed, but we are told in Deuteronomy 29:29, **The secret things belong unto the Lord our God.** We will not always know the whole story about each person who fails to receive his healing and goes home to be with the Lord. Perhaps pain drove the person to desire death, or a personal vision of heaven may have caused him to choose to depart for a far, far better place. Whatever the reason, we must let God's Word destroy strongholds in our thoughts so we can keep trusting Him and stay in a position to receive His blessings.

THE STRONGHOLD OF FEAR
• • •

Fear can force us to crumble before our adversary, opening the door in our lives to distress and disease. The following excerpts from Dr. David Yonggi Cho's books *The Fourth Dimension,* Volumes 1 and 2, provide a dramatic example of how fear can cause us to make a casualty covenant with sickness and disease.

> When I was a student in junior high school, one of the classes I went to had bottles of alcohol filled with bones and intestines. The sight of these bottles filled with bones and intestines frightened me.

One morning the biology teacher was teaching on the subject of tuberculosis. In those days there were no miracle drugs, and the teacher said if you ever had tuberculosis you would be dissipated, your insides looking like these bottles, the rest of your life.

He told of the dangers of tuberculosis and at the close said, "There are people who are born with a tendency to have tuberculosis. Men with narrow shoulders and long necks seem more apt to catch tuberculosis."

...In looking around I saw that I had the longest neck in my classroom. Right away I knew that I would get tuberculosis.[3]

Dr. Cho continues in his second volume,

During a normal afternoon, while I was tutoring a junior high school student, I felt very sick. My chest was heaving convulsively, and I began to vomit blood. After bleeding profusely from my mouth and nostrils, I fainted and collapsed.

...It did not take the doctors long to diagnose the trouble. I had advanced and terminal tuberculosis.... "You have three or four months to live," was the last thing the doctor told me as I was sent home.

...The calendar by my bed had only three months left on it. "Dear Buddha, won't you help me to get better and live?" I prayed daily. But nothing happened.... Then one day, I prayed a prayer that was to change my life. "Oh, unknown God, if You exist, please help me. If You can give me my life back, I promise You that I will spend the rest of my days serving You and helping others...."

Not long after my prayer to the One, True and Living God, a young lady came to visit me. The girl was in high school, and she came after school with a large book under her arm. "I want to speak with you about Jesus Christ, Yonggi," she said....

"Thank you for coming, but as you know, I am a good Buddhist. Since I am about to die, I would not consider changing religions," I responded to her as kindly as I could. She did not know how upset I really was.

"That's all right," she continued. "I am going to speak to you about Jesus anyway...."

I listened patiently to her strange story, but when she left I was relieved. The next day after school, there she was again....

Finally, after I had heard her story over and over again I lost my patience and told her to get lost. "Please, don't tell me any more. I'm sick and tired of your persistence and foolish stories; allow me to die in peace," I screamed in desperation.

I thought that my rudeness would drive her away. But she did not leave. Instead, she simply lowered her head by my bed and began to pray for me. Then she began to cry: "Please, Jesus, forgive him. He is sick; he does not mean what he is saying," she prayed, unable to hold back the tears. The sight of her kneeling and praying before me touched me very deeply.... Who is this God that she talks about so much that would send someone to spend every afternoon talking to me and sharing the concern that she shared? Could this girl's God be the God that I prayed to when I was begging for my life?

Suddenly, I felt a strange, tingling sensation. Goose bumps were all over my body. I was scared, confused, but also challenged. "Please stop crying," I begged as I touched her head. "I'm sorry I got so angry with you. I will become a Christian for your sake." With that, she looked up at me and began to smile....

"I want you to take my most prized possession," she said softly as she handed me her Bible....

This was the first time I had ever held a Bible in my hand. I found it rather large and cumbersome. Yet, with her assistance, I found the Gospel of Matthew, the beginning of the New Testament....

Still struggling with pain, I knelt down as my young friend had done when she had cried over me. Then I uttered the words that would revolutionize my whole life and affect my country:"Dear Jesus, please forgive me my sins. I am not worthy to belong to You. But if You can, accept me. I give myself to You. Please save me and heal me. Amen!" As I prayed I was unable to hold back the tears.

Suddenly, I felt clean. It was as if someone had given me a bath on the inside. I stood up and shouted, "Hallelujah! Thank You, God...."

...Without anyone telling me, I knew I was going to live. After the pages of my calendar were gone, I was still alive. In six months, I was able to get out of my bed, and I have not had trouble with tuberculosis since.[4]

Like attracts like, and like produces like. If you have fear, the devil has an open channel through which to come and strike you; fear is negative faith. So, as I feared tuberculosis, I contracted tuberculosis, and as I vomited blood I said to myself, "Yes, this is exactly as I expected."

...If a person has a specific fear, then the power of destruction begins to flow.[5]

In that biology classroom, fear caused young Yonggi Cho to make a covenant with disease. But later in his bedroom, faith delivered him, and that evil covenant was broken. Dr. David Yonggi Cho is currently pastor of the largest church in the world, located in Seoul, Korea.

Fear is a stronghold that will rob us of God's best for our lives. Therefore, we must renew our minds and change our thinking patterns to conform to God's Word, which is our bondage-breaker and freedom-maker. As we align our thoughts and conform our lives to the ultimate conqueror, the Lord Jesus Christ, we become conquerors ourselves. We ascend the "highway of holiness," rising above every demonic attempt to deceive us into making casualty covenants.

Remember, *the mind is the battleground, and fear is the foe!*

> **For ye have not received the spirit of bondage again to fear; but ye have received the Spirit of adoption, whereby we cry, Abba, Father.**
>
> **Romans 8:15**

GOD WANTS YOU WELL
• • •

We don't have to allow fear to destroy our faith; we need only know that God wants us well! I've seen this principle in action again and again, but one time in particular has always stuck out in my mind.

In our monthly Prayer Bibles Studies meetings, I regularly teach an interdenominational group. At the end of each meeting, we always pray with those who desire personal prayer, so I was not surprised when Sally came speedily forward for prayer.

Sally was a slender Southern lady and a good Bible student. I didn't know that for twenty years she had suffered with bouts of vertigo. Her most recent attack had been so severe that just the act of driving herself to the Prayer Bible Studies meeting that day had been difficult.

Although still suffering from the dizziness associated with vertigo, Sally seated herself in our big, blue "prayer chair" and asked us to pray that the Lord would heal her of this physical condition.

However, before I could begin to pray, I had a real check in my spirit. The Holy Spirit was alerting me that we were not yet ready to pray.

While questioning Sally, I discovered that she was struggling mentally with receiving healing. She explained that she had a relative in the hospital who was much more sick than she was.

Sally had done all she knew to do to help her relative receive healing. But the relative resisted all of Sally's suggestions, refusing to read any inspirational material or hear any helpful tapes on healing.

I listened to Sally recite her concern that perhaps she shouldn't be healed because her relative, whose condition was much more serious than her own, hadn't received healing. Sally's words left me wondering why she had forced herself to drive to the Prayer Bible Studies meeting or come forward for prayer. It sounded as if she had already made the choice to stay sick.

In hindsight, I realize we were witnessing a real spiritual battle being waged in Sally's mind. The demon of infirmity was staging a last-minute onslaught in her thoughts, using condemnation and false guilt tactics to deceive her. This demonic attack had established a stronghold in Sally's thought patterns, sending her on a tormenting guilt trip designed to take her as far away as possible from the Prayer Bible Studies, where she might receive help.

Satan wanted Sally to agree—to make a covenant— with him to hold on to her condition of vertigo. If she had actually done this, we could have prayed all day and still had no success. God had given Sally a free will;

He would let her choose whether or not she received her healing.

In other words, Satan told Sally that if she couldn't get her very sick relative healed, she—who was suffering from a much more minor illness—didn't deserve to be healed herself.

Perplexed at the time, I just looked to my Father God with silent prayer: *Lord, I'm not sufficient for this. What shall I do?* Faster than lightning strikes, I received His answer: *Tell her that her Father wants her well!*

I repeated those words to Sally in the exact authoritative tone with which I had heard them. Sally responded by nodding her head in agreement. She said, "If my Father wants me well, then I will have to be well!"

Then we laid hands on her and prayed for her total healing, commanding a spirit of infirmity to leave in Jesus' name. The Lord miraculously healed Sally of vertigo at that moment, and she has maintained her healing for many years.

God's particular pathway of healing for Sally is confirmed in Scripture:

> **Is any sick among you? let him call for the elders of the church; and let them pray over him, anointing him with oil in the name of the Lord: and the prayer of faith shall save the sick, and the Lord shall raise him up; and if he have committed sins, they shall be forgiven him.**
>
> **James 5:14,15**

SEE YOURSELF HEALED
. . .

Several years ago, I was invited to speak on God's healing power in a nearby city. I was delighted to accept. I knew what would happen when I ministered on the subject of healing. God's Word tells us that He will confirm His Word with signs following:

> **God also bearing them witness, both with signs and wonders, and with divers miracles, and gifts of the Holy Ghost, according to his own will.**
>
> **Hebrews 2:4**

That's why I love to teach on healing. Even though I am an ordinary person, I serve an extraordinary God whose power is always present to confirm His Word. He loves His creation with an everlasting love and desires to see each person made whole. Therefore, I am privileged to see Him perform healing miracles on a regular basis!

The morning of this particular meeting, I sensed an excitement and anticipation in the people. Faith had been building in their hearts from previous meetings that I had held in nearby churches.

After I had finished my message, "God Wants You Well," the people crowded the altar for prayer. The anointing was very strong. I moved quickly down the line of people, lightly laying a hand on each person's head. The Lord's power was present to heal, and everyone seemed to receive His healing touch.

Well, not quite everyone. As I moved down the healing line, I came to a beautiful woman seated in a chair who apparently had not received. This was a surprise, given the strong atmosphere of faith and the tangible presence of Jesus in the room.

I asked the woman to explain her condition and what the doctors had told her. She said she was handicapped and the doctors hadn't been able to help her. Looking at her legs, I observed that one leg was about three inches shorter than the other. The shorter leg was the size of a broomstick, whereas her other leg appeared to be of normal size.

I decided to specifically pray for this woman and to command spirits of infirmity to leave her. Nothing happened. I prayed silently to God, asking, *What is this woman's problem, Lord?*

The answer came immediately as the Holy Spirit spoke to my spirit: *She sees herself crippled. Ask her if she can see herself healed by the power of God.*

Fixing my eyes upon the woman, I asked her the question. With our eyes locked together, she answered with conviction, *"Yes!"* As soon as that response of faith came out of her mouth, the short leg jumped out about three inches to match the length of the normal leg. The onlookers gasped with astonishment. The woman's healing had begun!

How Do You See Yourself?

The Lord's question to this woman is an important one for each of us to answer. How we see ourselves internally can affect us externally. Our Creator wants us to be healthy, but much depends on whether or not we allow our own mental images of ourselves to help us or hurt us.

For example, when I was dying of cancer, I purchased a pair of pink pumps. They were a symbol of renewed health and vigor to me, reminding me of the time I would be free again to move about in my own strength. This mental image encouraged me to believe for my full recovery.

It is so important for you to understand how God sees you in Christ. Remember, Proverbs 23:7 says that as a person thinks in his heart, so is he.

A study of God's Word will help you form a clear, scriptural mental image of yourself. It will also help you discover and break any covenants you have made about yourself with that old thief, the devil.

So how do you see yourself?

- Can you see yourself healed?

- Can you see yourself forgiven and born again, with Christ, the hope of glory, dwelling within?

- Can you see yourself clothed in His righteousness?

- Can you see yourself receiving the benefits of the covenant you have with God? (Remember, Psalm 103:2-3 RSV says, **Bless the Lord, O my soul, and forget not all his benefits, who forgives all your iniquities, who heals all your diseases.**)

- Can you see yourself reading, hearing and believing God's Word?

- Can you see yourself exercising the faith God has already given you?

- Can you see yourself forgiving others by your own decision?

- Can you see yourself successful and healthy in spirit, soul and body?

We must dwell on God's positive thoughts about us. In Christ we can do all things that our Lord has planned and purposed for us to do. (Phil. 4:13; Eph. 2:10.) However, we must be diligent to resist the devil and all his negative thoughts so he will flee from us! (James 4:7.)

MIRACLES IN COSTA RICA

I remember the time I learned firsthand how dangerous it can be to one's health to make a false covenant with fear. Interestingly, this hard lesson occurred after experiencing a very successful ministry trip to Costa Rica.

About a month before I was to depart for ministry in Costa Rica, I joined with another Christian in prayer concerning the messages I was to give in that nation. One of the meetings planned for this trip was a miracle service in the Templo Biblico of San José. As my friend and I prayed, I clearly understood that the Lord wanted me to preach a message on creative miracles at this particular service.

After arriving in San José, I chose to do some additional Bible study on God's creative miracles. Then the night before the miracle service, the Lord prompted me to include Mark 7:32-35. In this passage of Scripture, Jesus commanded a deaf and mute spirit to leave a man, and immediately the man was healed.

On the appointed day of the miracle service, I stood behind the pulpit and looked out at the packed church auditorium. The balcony was completely filled, and people stood against the side walls. Only the Holy Spirit could minister to such a great multitude of people.

As I finished my message on creative miracles, I knew in my spirit that I was to leave the pulpit, descend the platform steps and begin to walk down the center aisle toward the church entryway to minister. But when I was midway down the aisle, a woman stood up in the middle of one of the rows and began shrieking. Glancing briefly at the woman, I knew this was a manifestation of witch-craft. I also sensed that if I stopped to deal with this woman, I would move outside of God's will because the Holy Spirit was still prompting me to continue my walk down the center aisle.

The devil had planned to distract me from finding the person God had appointed for me to minister to. If I had agreed to this tactic, I would have missed God's plan. (How many victories does Satan win by distracting us from the real purposes of God?)

From the corner of my eye, I saw two men lift the stiff-ened form of the woman from the row of seats and take her out of the church. Meanwhile, I continued to proceed peacefully toward the end of the aisle.

Suddenly I came to a woman, a doctor's wife, who spoke English. This woman had received permission to bring a little eight-year-old boy who was deaf and mute to the miracle service.

As I stood there with the woman and the little boy, I knew exactly what to do. I had never seen the woman or the boy before, nor had I any prior knowledge that I would meet them in the church. But God had orchestrated the whole "happening," starting with the time of prayer we'd had in Houston, Texas.

Because I had dodged the enemy's earlier attempt to get me to agree with the spirit of distraction, all I had to do was obey the Holy Spirit. I recalled the night before, when the Holy Spirit had led me to Mark 7:32-35:

And they bring unto him one that was deaf, and had an impediment in his speech; and they beseech him to put his hand upon him.

And he took him aside from the multitude, and put his fingers into his ears, and he spit, and touched his tongue; and looking up to heaven, he sighed, and saith unto him, Ephphatha, that is, Be opened. And straightway his ears were opened, and the string of his tongue was loosed, and he spake plain.

In obedience to the Scriptures, I followed Jesus' pattern to deliver the eight-year-old from a deaf and mute spirit. Then I released the boy to my Spanish translator for observation and headed back toward the pulpit.

Before I had managed even a few steps through the crowd that was now pressing in around us, the translator returned with the boy, exclaiming, "He is hearing! He is speaking!"

We quickly taught the boy to say "Jesus" and "Hallelujah!" The woman who brought him could not stop weeping for joy. There seemed to be a fountain of water gushing from her eyes! The whole church joined together in mighty thanksgiving and praise to our Creator, the God of miracles!

There were many other divine gifts of healings and miracles that day in the church and throughout Costa Rica in the days that followed as Almighty God blessed the people in our miracle services. I returned to Texas with great joy and gratitude for all His benefits and blessings.

FROM FEAR TO FAITH TO VICTORY
. . .

The next time I was invited to minister in Costa Rica and Panama, I felt some hesitation. How could this second trip possibly be as great as the last one? However, because I was very busy with services in the United States, I didn't have much time to dwell on these apprehensive thoughts.

On this second trip to Latin America, I planned to take two Christian friends to help. I was also looking forward to working with those in Central America who had invited us.

As I rushed from one appointment to another in the days before the scheduled trip, I developed a cough that disturbed my sleep and caused pain in my chest. At first, I paid no attention to it. But finally, I decided to see a physician, hoping for some medication with a quick cure.

When the doctor had examined the results of my X ray, he surprised me with some unexpected news: "Mrs. Winborn, you have pneumonia." This explained the coughing and the unexpected fatigue that had plagued me for weeks.

I realized that my plans for an extended ministry trip into Costa Rica would have to be canceled. I also needed to inform the two ladies who were planning to travel with me of my condition. I had just returned from the clinic with doctor's orders to go home and stay in bed. I needed a miracle!

I immediately called my traveling companions so they could cancel their airline reservations. As I explained my situation, I sensed their disappointment.

I pondered how to break the news to my missionary friend in Costa Rica. She would have to cancel all the church meetings and miracle services she had scheduled for me. I felt badly that I couldn't keep my word to her.

My phone call went right through to San José, and the missionary answered the call. I told her, "I have pneumonia and am unable to come to Costa Rica. You will have to cancel all the meetings you have arranged for me."

My missionary friend didn't miss a beat. She replied, "No, I will not cancel the meetings, because you *will* come."

Thinking she must have misunderstood the seriousness of the sickness, I explained it all to her once more. She said, "The ladies are here now for a prayer meeting. We will pray for you, and you will come."

Such a strong statement of faith surprised me. After talking with the missionary, I considered her challenge to stand in faith for my trip to Costa Rica. I might have been down, but I wasn't out! The will to fight began to rise up within me.

As I looked unto the Lord, I was impressed with the thought, *Call Francis* [she was a powerful woman of God I knew]. *She is having a prayer meeting. Explain the circumstances to her and ask for prayer.* Although I had forgotten about Francis' prayer meeting, the Lord had not.

When I called Francis, she promised immediate prayer coverage. Afterwards, I lay on my bed and considered these developments. Faith was stirring in my heart.

God seemed to be drawing from two powerful prayer sources—two strong sources of light—one in Houston, Texas, and the other in San José, Costa Rica. As I drifted off to sleep, I knew something had to give. Warfare prayer was happening on my behalf, and heaven was hearing!

In Betty Malz's book *Prayers That Are Answered*, she had this to say about the power of prevailing prayer:

> During my death and out-of-the-body experience, I stood in His presence and witnessed prayer in the form of direct, pulsating shafts of light, joining the great light in Heaven's Throne Room. I am confident of the power of prayer. Since then, when I stand or kneel in prayer, I feel that same power and know that there is not unbridgeable distance between earth and Heaven—from man to God. I have seen the other end of prayer. We may stand on earth and pray in faith and confidence believing that the answer will come.[6]

Awakening the next morning, I realized that I hadn't coughed during the night. Gazing in the mirror, I noticed that some color had returned to my face. It began to dawn on me that I felt perfectly fine!

Switching on the television set, I began to watch a program on the Christian Broadcasting Network. A beautiful blonde woman on the program was operating in the gift of the word of knowledge. Suddenly she said, "There is a woman watching this program who has had a problem with her lungs." She seemed to look at me from the television screen, and she said, "You are healed."

I grabbed hold of that word by faith and replied, "Thank you very much, Lord!"

Then I prayed, *Lord, when you healed Simon Peter's mother-in-law, she got up and immediately began to serve.* [Mark 1:30,31.] *I want to go to Costa Rica and serve You.*

Dressing swiftly, I drove to the clinic and had another X ray. This time there was no sign of pneumonia!

Next I called my two friends, who immediately rescheduled their airline reservations. Finally, I called the missionary and told her we would all be there in time for the scheduled meetings. (As it turned out, I only missed one.)

When we arrived in San José, the missionary and another precious friend met us at the airport. They told me that as they had prayed for me, they had been impressed with the Scripture about Peter's mother-in-law arising and serving others immediately after she was healed. This wonderful confirmation reassured me that I was in the right place at the right time.

In retrospect, I remembered my concerned thoughts: *Would the miracles be as great on this second trip to Central America as they had been on the first one? Was I still flowing with the Holy Spirit in creative miracles?* At the time, I didn't realize that the cold edge of fear had knifed its way through my shield of faith.

Fear is the opposite force from faith, and Romans 14:23 warns, **Whatsoever is not of faith is sin.** Fear had penetrated my spiritual armor for battle, resulting in an open door for the spirit of infirmity to enter and harass me with pneumonia. I made this covenant with fear on an unconscious level, but it was sufficient to

BREAKING CASUALTY COVENANTS

make me physically vulnerable to an attack from Satan's evil empire.

The good news is that prevailing prayer by the body of Jesus Christ caused the devil to give way, and I was healed through their prayers!

He will even deliver the one [for whom you intercede] who is not innocent; yes, he will be delivered through the cleanness of your hands.

Job 22:30 AMP

In natural warfare, a soldier fights alongside his fellow soldiers to bring down strongholds. It is the same in spiritual warfare. We need the prayers of other believers. We cannot afford a "Lone Ranger" mentality.

The enemy had conned me into fearing that God would not be present to heal as mightily as before, and that unconscious covenant with fear seriously affected my health. However, in reality, more miracles occurred on the second trip than on the first, because I enlisted the missionary and her prayer team as helpers and received prayer support from Christian groups in Texas as well. Prayer changes things!

As President Franklin D. Roosevelt once said, "There is nothing to fear but fear itself." Fear opens the door to casualty covenants, but the power of faith-filled prayer can break those wrong covenants and take you on to victory!

THE POWER OF FERVENT PRAYER
• • •

I had to trust in God's answer to my own fervent prayers for my mother one time when she lay close to death. As I prayed for her, I received a word from the Lord that helped me keep standing for her healing in the face of Satan's strategy to deceive.

As long as I can remember, my mother constantly suffered from severe headaches. I can still see her in my mind's eye, sitting on her bed, holding her head in her hands as she struggled with another sinus headache.

Problems with sinus infections are common in people living near the Gulf Coast of Texas. So, thinking that her headaches were an inevitable part of living in that region, Mother just endured the pain and discomfort until they passed.

Mother was never a complainer; neither did she spend much time in self-pity. But as the years went by, her headaches became more excruciating, so she sought a cure from many able physicians.

I recall taking her to a succession of doctors who filled her medicine cabinet with prescription medicines. One doctor even told her to hang by her chin for a specified time each day! I suppose he thought her problem was in her muscles and that by stretching her neck, she would get better.

However, none of the doctors were really able to help my mother. And although my prayers comforted her, the headaches continued. She was worn out with the problem, and so was I. I was also concerned that she was taking too much pain medication.

Then we learned that my mother's sister, Helen, was coming to visit her. I hoped that perhaps the pleasure of my aunt's visit would help alleviate Mother's headaches.

Mother always enjoyed dressing up and keeping up with the latest beauty treatments. So in anticipation of my Aunt Helen's visit, Mother went to the beauty salon to get her hair styled and made dinner reservations for a special evening of celebration. Mother's husband went along with it all, thankful for the diversion my aunt's visit would provide for both of them.

Although I wasn't in the city for this happy occasion, I knew I'd be close enough to drive home in a few hours if necessary. The respite would be good for all of us.

Aunt Helen arrived, and the three of them prepared to leave the house for their special evening. But before they could depart, Mother was suddenly struck with blinding pain in her head. Then one of her eyes began to droop involuntarily.

Mother's pain was so intense that her husband and Aunt Helen rushed her to the hospital's emergency room. Unbeknownst to them (but not to God!), the hospital they chose was the only one in Houston at the time with the equipment necessary to determine her problem!

All these years, we had thought Mother's problem was her sinuses. In truth, it was a swollen blood vessel in her head—an aneurysm!

Mother's condition was so serious that surgery was planned for the next morning. An intern was assigned to watch her all night in case the swollen blood vessel burst.

Rushing back to Houston and the hospital, I could hardly believe this sudden turn of events. There was no way to control my mother's care. We were totally dependent on the expertise of the hospital medical staff.

After arriving at the hospital, I found a place where I could be alone. Dropping to my knees, I began to pray fervently to the Great Physician for my mother's life. She was in her sixties, yet she was still only a baby in Christ. Just recently, she had invited Jesus into her life, so I knew she was one of His. But she still didn't know how to defend herself against Satan, who obviously planned to take her life!

As I prayed, the Holy Spirit spoke these words in my spirit: *She will be all right.*

Mother survived the surgery. Afterwards, she lay unconscious in the intensive care room. Each day I went to see her, even though she didn't know I was there. Her right side was paralyzed, and the doctors said her speech might be permanently impaired. With all the faith I had, I hung on to the words the Lord had given me.

One day as I walked up to the intensive care receptionist's desk, I noticed that a new nurse was sitting there. I was a little early for my allotted visiting time, so I stopped and, without identifying myself, asked her about the condition of the woman who had undergone aneurysm surgery.

The nurse replied, "Oh, that woman is dead." At my look of alarm, she qualified her statement, saying, "Well, she is almost dead; she won't last much longer."

Staring at this "bad news" receptionist, the devil's advocate, I realized she was totally ignorant of her misconduct. She didn't know she was speaking to the woman's daughter, who had received a promise from God.

I suddenly understood that this was a trick of the devil to cause me to agree—to make a covenant—with her prophecy of death for my mother. At the zero hour of Mother's recovery, Satan was firing his last attempt to rob her of life by robbing me of faith for her healing.

I made no reply to the receptionist. Now aware of the enemy's strategy, I just ignored the evil prognosis and walked away from the desk as quickly as possible.

I went to my mother's bedside. She was still unconscious. I laid my hands on her head in prayer and began to thank God for her full recovery. I rebuked the paralysis, the speech impairment and all complications in the name of Jesus Christ, the King of kings and Lord of lords.

As I stood beside Mother's unconscious form, very quietly I began to sing a song of praise and adoration to a merciful God. I made no covenant with the devil regarding my mother's life. Instead, I declared, "She will live and not die!"

I believed it was Almighty God who had impressed me with those words concerning my mother: *She will be all right.* Now I was holding fast to His promise to me. My mother was unconscious and unable to choose for herself, so I would stand in the gap for her.

Later that evening, the family was all together at the hospital. As we waited for the physician to come and talk to us, my mother suddenly regained consciousness! She was even able to speak clearly. And within a matter of days, the paralysis in her side had disappeared.

Although we knew that God had miraculously healed Mother from the effects of the aneurysm, we also appreciated the good medical care she had received. Soon after being released from the hospital, she regained her strength and suffered no more complications or headaches.

According to the word of the Lord, Mother was indeed all right!

Mother lived many more years, giving all thanks to God, her Creator.

Of course, Isaiah 55:11 assures us:

So shall my word be that goeth forth out of my mouth: it shall not return unto me void, but it shall accomplish that which I please, and it shall prosper in the thing whereto I sent it.

LAUGHTER IS GOOD MEDICINE!

Another personal experience again taught me a way we can make a casualty covenant with the enemy and open the door to sickness in our lives. This experience started innocently enough with a visit to a doctor, but it could have ended in disaster if I had not recognized a new twist to the devil's deceptive devices.

Because the Lord is faithful to confirm His Word with signs and wonders, we regularly see His miracles in our monthly Prayer Bible Studies. We started this study in 1976 to share God's Word primarily with Catholics. Even though it has since become interdenominational, we are still blessed to have some of the original members attending.

Years ago, one of these original members shared with me her concern for her neighbor, who had cancer. Knowing that a great deal of faith is always present for miracles in our Prayer Bible Studies, I suggested that my friend bring her neighbor to one of the meetings so the woman could receive encouragement and prayer for healing.

On the appointed day, my friend introduced Grace, her neighbor, to me right after the Bible teaching. Grace requested that I pray for her.

As I laid my hand on her left side, I was surprised at the intensity of heat in my hand. Grace exclaimed, "Oh, your hand is so hot—I can feel it burning into my side where the cancer is located!"

After such a strong manifestation of the power of the Holy Spirit to heal, we expected a good report from Grace's physician. We were not disappointed; Grace was much improved. However, as time passed, I wondered why we didn't hear more from her, given the fact that the Lord had touched her so dramatically.

Later I found out that Grace's daughter had been seeing a physician who diagnosed nutritional needs. His approach and tests were different from others'. Grace's daughter took her to this physician so he could help her with her diet. Grace began to sing the doctor's praises, giving him credit for her healing.

I wondered if perhaps this doctor's nutritional advice was a part of her recovery. I decided I would check him out. I felt I could use more energy, and since diet is so important to good health, I wanted to learn more about eating correctly.

When I arrived for my appointment at this physician's office, I found him to be a nice man. He shared that he was discouraged because other doctors did not appreciate his advanced methods of diagnosing diseases. Then he reviewed my medical records, noting the history of terminal cancer. In answer to his questions, I told him that I had received a miracle of healing. He made no comment.

After studying the results of a few tests he had taken, the doctor prescribed various vitamins and minerals for me to take and suggested I come again for further tests.

At the next appointment, the doctor conducted more tests. One of them was designed to gauge my physical strength. The doctor instructed me to resist him as he tried to push my right arm down toward my side. Next, he put a packet of sugar in my right hand. Then as I held the sugar, he once again instructed me to resist as he pushed down on my right arm.

Evidently, this test proves that sugar is bad for you, because there seems to be less strength to resist when you are holding a sugar packet in your hand. This method of testing is used in kinesiology, the study of human muscular movements.

The doctor was also studying a procedure that diagnosed a person's condition by looking at the iris— the round, pigmented membrane surrounding the pupil of the eye.

Suddenly, the doctor startled me by exclaiming, "You have heart trouble!" I assured him that I did *not* have heart trouble. He then said, "You have Epstein-Barr."

I replied, "No, I do not have Epstein-Barr." (At this time, Epstein-Barr was a popular diagnosis. One of the symptoms is excessive fatigue.) I was beginning to understand why this doctor was being criticized by other doctors!

Then later in the examination, the doctor gave me a new diagnosis: "You have cancer," he proclaimed.

I firmly responded, "Doctor, I do *not* have cancer!" (He didn't know that after my miraculous healing of terminal cancer, I had gone to my doctor for annual checkups, all of which disclosed no trace of cancer.)

This entire examination was becoming so ludicrous that suddenly I burst out laughing. My laughter seemed to set the doctor back a bit. I didn't want to be disrespectful, but I couldn't stop laughing.

Also, I perceived that the enemy was using this physician to deceive me into making a casualty covenant by believing and receiving the doctor's false diagnoses.

Still laughing, I said, "Doctor, don't you understand? If I had all those diseases, I couldn't have even driven myself here to keep this appointment with you!"

That statement slowed him down, but he had one more shot to fire. He said, "You have tuberculosis."

I replied, "I do *not* have tuberculosis!"

He said, "Yes, you do."

I looked at this man, a possible charlatan, and asked, "Isn't there an accepted patch test that you use to diagnose TB?" (An idea was forming in my mind. Perhaps, if I could prove to this man that his diagnosis was wrong, he would realize that he was being deceived and that he wasn't going to deceive me.)

The doctor replied that there was such a patch test. I suggested he give me this test for TB. He reluctantly found the patch test, applied it to my arm and told me to come back in two weeks.

I left with the TB patch test on my arm, totally positive I didn't have the disease. But I was hoping the outcome would convince the doctor that his tests were false and could get him in big trouble if he continued to use them to diagnose his patients.

As I drove away, I couldn't help chuckling. Stopping at another Christian's home, I briefly shared about the TB prognosis, explaining the patch on my arm. I laughingly included some of the other diseases I was supposed to have.

That night, I slept soundly, except for one surprise. Laughter kept waking me up in the middle of the night! After a second or so, I'd realize that it was *my* laughter. I was even laughing in my sleep! This occurred several times throughout the night.

I had never done that before, nor have I done it since. Is it possible that the Holy Spirit was the source of my laughter? I believe so.

We know that the Holy Spirit resides in the believer's spirit. Scripture says, **The Lord is laughing at those who plot against the godly, for he knows their judgment day is coming** (Ps. 37:12,13 TLB). So every time I woke up laughing, it was as if I was laughing at the devil by the unction of the Holy Spirit within!

Through this experience, I learned the truth of Proverbs 17:22: **A merry heart doeth good like a medicine.** Even though I had to pay for all the medical tests this doctor conducted, it was worth it to receive this gift of laughter!

THE DANGER OF A FALSE DIAGNOSIS
* * *

When I returned two weeks later to see the doctor, he removed the patch. There was no evidence of tuberculosis. However, he just claimed he had used an inferior patch. (He probably feared a malpractice suit.) I silently prayed for him and departed.

Sadly, the woman who had cancer and had trusted in this same doctor to heal her ended up dying from her disease.

The purpose of this illustration is to sound the alert about false medical diagnoses. The devil was trying to get me to agree with a false diagnosis so I would eventually accept cancer in my body again.

A false medical diagnosis is dangerous. If we believe and accept it, we can become entangled in a casualty covenant. Just because the source of the diagnosis is credible doesn't necessarily mean it's correct.

The Holy Spirit can give you discernment on these matters. It may be necessary to break a diagnostic curse over you or others by using the name of Jesus Christ, which represents His authority and His righteousness.

A FLAT STOMACH, A MILLION DOLLARS OR TRUE FAITH?

• • •

When my granddaughter was a young college student, she was so helped by learning about casualty covenants that she decided to share this knowledge with another young woman. My granddaughter related the incident to me:

> My very attractive, educated friend, who is a fitness buff, received this information gladly. She had just been working out at the gym. As she patted her tummy, she smiled and said, "You are telling me that all I have to do is keep telling myself my stomach will be flat—and it will!"
>
> A little alarmed at her misunderstanding of my words, I laughed and said, "That's not quite the way it works."

Immediately upon hearing the principle of casualty covenants, my granddaughter's friend made the *mental* connection. However, she didn't make a heart, or a *spiritual,* connection.

That's why it's important to understand that there is a natural realm, in which humans live, and a spiritual realm, where angels and demons exist. Born-again humans are to walk in the realm of the Holy Spirit, who indwells their spirits. As they walk in obedience to God's Word, they also operate in the supernatural power of the Holy Spirit.

Almighty God hears our prayers. James 5:16 says, **The effectual fervent prayer of a righteous man availeth much.** But in order to experience God's best in every area of life, including our health, we need to get beyond our senses and move over into God's realm—the realm of faith in His Word.

In this realm, saying scriptural words is necessary, but it is not enough. For instance, just saying with your mouth that you will receive a million dollars does not open the door for you to, say, instantly inherit a bunch of money. Likewise, just repeating over and over, "I don't have this sickness in my body," isn't going to heal you. It is when your heart believes what your mouth is saying that obstacles will move. It's a heart *and* soul thing!

You see, without the right heart motive or enduring faith in God's Word, our words are about as worthless as a broken arrow.

The Holy Spirit will quicken a *rhema* Scripture—the spoken Word—to us from the *logos,* or the written Word of God. Then He helps our spirits to hold on tenaciously to this specific Scripture in true faith.

True, some people who rely on the natural realm could earn a million dollars or be diagnosed with a terminal disease and live to tell about it. But it's important to understand that God is not a God of luck. He is a covenant God of *promises*. But His people enjoy the benefits of those promises only as they learn to agree with *Him* rather than with the lies of the enemy.

So be sure that you never unwittingly make covenants with the devil—through fear or anything else—that would affect your health. Find out what God's Word says about healing, and agree with that!

God says His Word does not return to Him void. (Isa. 55:11.) As you set yourself in agreement with that anointed Word, it will accomplish in your life what He has sent it forth to do, bringing life, strength, healing and victory!

7

FORGIVENESS
BRINGS FREEDOM

Some of the most dangerous casualty covenants are the ones we make with bitterness and unforgiveness. When we allow bitterness to take root, it can bring destruction to every area of our lives—our mental and physical health, our relationships with others, our emotional well-being and our walk with God.

But we can live free from the self-destructive patterns of holding grudges and taking offense. Through the power of God's forgiving love, which is shed abroad in our hearts, we can break any covenants we have made with bitterness.

BITTERNESS: OUR OWN WORST ENEMY

The act of forgiving someone may be instantaneous or progressive, or it may never occur at all. As we struggle with the thoughts of how unjustly and unfairly we have been treated, we sometimes choose self-pity, self-righteousness or bitterness instead of God's way of forgiveness.

When we clothe ourselves in these dark "garments," spiritually we look like someone in mourning who is preparing to attend a funeral. And if we maintain an attitude of unforgiveness for too long, we may actually end up attending a real funeral—our own!

We must grasp the importance of forgiveness! Our health depends on it.

When we refuse to forgive, we bind ourselves to a person or a situation by a strong, negative emotional cord. Physicians are now recognizing that invisible cord as the link between ill health and prolonged bitterness and unforgiveness. That's why it's so important that we forgive—not only for the other person's sake, but for our own!

Forgiveness is difficult for us as human beings. We want justice. We want our own point of view to be vindicated. So we hold on to our expectations of being proven right, feeling justified in not forgiving an offender. We don't want to wait on God to make the situation right. We want justice *now*—preferably last month!

In Psalm 109, David expresses some of these same human emotions. This particular psalm isn't pretty. David is honest with God. He wants revenge. But he isn't to avenge himself; he is seeking *God* to do it.

In verse 22, David speaks of his wounded heart. He is hurting emotionally: **For I am poor and needy, and my heart is wounded within me.**

Negative emotions, such as resentment and self-pity, can cause us to fall into unforgiveness. The truth is, all of us have been hurt at one time or another. Usually, these wounds come from those we love and trust. This hurt makes us vulnerable to bitterness.

If we allow bitterness to fester in our hearts, we will begin to spew hateful, backbiting and malicious words out of our mouths, poisoning others and the atmosphere around us. Talk about environmental pollution! Bitterness can defile marriages, families and entire nations.

FORGIVENESS COMES FROM THE HEART

We can deceive ourselves by mentally agreeing that we *should* forgive, when our hearts are not in it. But God looks into our hearts; He is never deceived.

We need to understand that we will never be free ourselves until we forgive those who have offended us *from the depths of our hearts*. Halfhearted forgiveness is not spiritual forgiveness.

Often we are afraid to release our offenders by forgiving them because we don't want them in our lives again. But fear always brings bondage, and this particular fear is ungrounded because "Though forgiveness restores heart affection, in all cases relationships will not be restored *positionally*."[1]

We must choose to forgive in obedience in order to receive personal inner healing. Forgiveness of others and of ourselves is the bottom line if we are ever going to find healing and wholeness within.

REFUSE TO STAY BITTER

I know a woman who, after her husband deserted her for another woman, thought of ways to destroy the offenders. After all, they had committed adultery. They were sinning, and she was suffering!

However, as she contemplated the vengeful deeds she could do, she finally realized that she would never know when to stop. Suddenly the word of the Lord came to her through a Scripture that rose up from her spirit: **Beloved, never avenge yourselves, but leave it to the wrath of God; for it is written, "Vengeance is mine, I will repay, says the Lord"** (Rom. 12:19 RSV).

This woman chose to obey God and deliver herself from becoming a bitter woman instead of agreeing with a spirit of bitterness to curse her husband. She refused to make a casualty covenant. In the grace that God gives, she released her anger and pain to the One who cares for her; she took herself out of Satan's snare of unforgiveness and found peace in her soul.

This example proves you can escape making a casualty covenant with bitterness, even when the sin of another breaks your heart and dims your dreams.

A psychiatric nurse from Spokane, Washington, once related to me the many marital problems she had seen arising out of bitterness. She told me, "Many people are having physical and mental problems from broken marriages. They are embittered and afraid to ever again trust anyone in a relationship."

First John 4:18 gives us a solution to that type of situation: **There is no fear in love; but perfect love casteth out fear: because fear hath torment.** Forgiveness delivers us from the bondage of fear, setting us free to love again.

You can shipwreck your faith on the banks of resentment and retaliation. And you must be careful not to slip into the dark waters of unforgiveness and bitterness. The two, mixed with self-pity, can cause you to make wrong decisions and faulty judgments.

People who are ruled by these destructive emotions are not mentally sound. In fact, the Bible says that hatred is really murder in God's eyes. (Matt. 5:21,22.) With that in mind, Revelation 21:8 hits dangerously close to home to the person who goes through life refusing to forgive: **But the fearful...and murderers...shall have their part in the lake which burneth with fire and brimstone: which is the second death.**

What are we supposed to do about those who hurt us? Jesus gave us divine guidelines: **But I tell you, Love your enemies and pray for those who persecute you** (Matt. 5:44 AMP). We are to *pray* for those who curse us!

The apostle Stephen prayed for his persecutors before they killed him. His prayer of forgiveness released one of his persecutors, Saul, to later become Saint Paul. (Acts 7:60.)

When we receive the life and nature of the Lord Jesus Christ into our spirits, we receive the same Lord who spoke of forgiveness from the Cross.

Are we going to follow the way of our Lord, who prayed from the Cross, "Forgive them, Father, for they know not what they do"? (Luke 23:34.) Or are we going to follow the way of Cain, who vengefully murdered his brother Abel? (Gen. 4:8.)

The choice is ours!

FORGIVE IN ORDER TO BE FORGIVEN

You need to understand that if you do not forgive, you yourself do not receive forgiveness. Jesus made this very plain:

Your heavenly Father will forgive you if you forgive those who sin against you; but if you refuse to forgive them, he will not forgive you.

Matthew 6:14,15 TLB

To receive healing and freedom for ourselves, we must forgive all others—whether they are dead or alive—of every offense. But not only must we forgive others as God has forgiven us; we must also forgive *ourselves*.

Above all, we must refuse to become bitter against God. Satan is the source of affliction. He does his dirty work and then seeks to convince us that the evil results are God's fault. God is a good God, and He loves us. He does *not* work against His own creation.

What about those who have hurt the innocent, who have destroyed lives, who have wrought havoc on the earth? Romans 12:19 RSV still applies: **Vengeance is mine, I will repay, says the Lord.** No matter what the offense, you are never to take revenge on the offender out of bitterness and hatred. You must forgive if you want to be forgiven.

WE REAP WHAT WE SOW

People who choose to break the Creator's principles and laws suffer the consequences that inevitably result.

His own iniquities shall ensnare the wicked man, and he shall be held with the cords of his sin.

Proverbs 5:22 AMP

For whatever a man sows, that and that only is what he will reap.

Galatians 6:7 AMP

We can see an example of this spiritual principle by examining an incident involving the Italian Mafia. After some Mafia members were murdered, their bodies were examined by pathologists. The autopsy reports described all kinds of diseased organs in the dead men's bodies—obviously a direct result of the constant stress under which they lived.[2]

The law of sowing and reaping is an immutable spiritual law. An offender can refuse to repent of, or turn away from, his sin, or he can choose to practice sin on a continuing basis and retain the same sinful attitude or lifestyle. But if he makes the wrong choice, he opens himself up to demonic attacks and brings a curse upon himself, reaping the eventual consequences of his own iniquities in his body, in his mind and in the affairs of this life. (1 Cor. 5:5.)

On the other hand, if the sinner confesses his sins with heartfelt repentance, God is faithful and just to forgive. (1 John 1:9.) However, the sinner, although forgiven, still may have to suffer some of the consequences of his sins while alive on planet earth.

As long as we dwell on this planet, we are subject to sin. I once heard someone say, "Satan doesn't have to lead me into temptation—I can find it myself!" But God doesn't tempt us. We are led astray by our own lusts—the lusts of the flesh, the lust of the eyes and the pride of life. (1 John 2:16.)

It is humbling to know that King David, the psalmist of God, committed adultery, conspired to have a man killed and then deceived himself about the sinfulness of his situation. (2 Sam. 11,12.) But when David repented, God forgave him. (Ps. 51:1-4.) Nonetheless, David reaped the natural consequences of his sin, experiencing serious family troubles for the rest of his life.

GOD'S FORGIVENESS VS. SATAN'S CONDEMNATION

When we fall into any kind of sin or miss the mark of obeying our Lord and Savior, we need to immediately ask for forgiveness and deliberately turn away from the indiscretion. We can ask for God's mercy because the Bible says His mercies are new every morning. (Lam. 3:22,23.) Also, Psalm 103:9 NAS says, **He will not always strive with us; nor will He keep His anger forever.**

The Lord tells us that when we repent, He will not remind us of our sins. In fact, He will forget them.

For You have cast all my sins behind Your back.

Isaiah 38:17 AMP

For I will be merciful and gracious toward their sins and I will remember their deeds of unrighteousness no more.

Hebrews 8:12 AMP

136

You are not to live in the past. This doesn't mean you must have a memory lapse. But it does mean that past sins have no more dominion over you. You are delivered from their poison.

On the other hand, the accuser of our souls sends a spirit of condemnation to torment us about the past. Satan seeks to keep us in condemnation. He knows that if he succeeds, he can prevent us from coming boldly before our Father God in prayer. Thus, he renders us ineffective in promoting the kingdom of God and keeps us from living an abundant life.

Now, which example do you want to pattern your life after—the unconditional forgiveness of Almighty God, or the bitter condemnation of the enemy?

DROP THE OFFENSE
· · ·

Once as I was ministering in a Texas town to a long line of people desiring personal prayer, a woman asked me, "Mickie, how do you forgive?"

I had just taught briefly on forgiveness and was therefore surprised at her question. Feeling too fatigued to give her another teaching, I silently prayed to the Lord for an answer to her question. Swiftly the thought came: *Hand her a book.*

Turning to the pulpit behind me, I reached for a book and handed it to her. As I waited for the Holy Spirit's leading, I heard these words in my spirit: *Tell her to drop it!*

As I delivered the Lord's message to her, she looked at me with trepidation and then dropped the book. It hit the floor with a loud thud.

The next heavenly instruction came immediately: *That's how you forgive—you drop it!*

Luke 6:37 AMP says, **Acquit and forgive and release (give up resentment, *let it drop*), and you will be acquitted and forgiven and released.** This simple formula for forgiveness works! I cannot tell you how many times those words have set people free.

A friend of mine thought this illustration of forgiveness was so helpful that she taught it to her Sunday school class for six-year-olds. After class, she overheard two little boys outside the schoolroom discussing the lesson. One little boy said to the other, "How did she say you forgive?"

After pondering this for a minute, the second little boy answered, "You get a book, and you drop it!"

(It lost something in the translation, didn't it?)

ASK FOR GRACE TO FORGIVE
• • •

As Christians, we have the life of Jesus within us. Therefore, we can draw from the Lord's divine ability to forgive. If we need special grace from Him to walk in forgiveness, all we have to do is ask Him for it. He understands our heartaches.

Corrie ten Boom was a member of a Dutch family of devout Christians who hid Jews in their house during the Nazi occupation of World War II. Because of their underground work, they were eventually discovered, captured by the Nazis and put in a concentration camp. Corrie survived and for many years traveled the world with a ministry of comfort and counsel. In her book *Marching Orders for the End Battle,* Corrie wrote about the subject of forgiveness:

> Sometimes we need a little grindstone to polish our character.... I had started a work for which I had a great love in my heart, but my friends, who in fact carried out this work for me because I was always travelling, could not agree with the aim and with my way of bringing the gospel. Then they asked me to withdraw and to give them a free hand. I became angry, and bitterness came into my heart. I confessed it immediately to the Lord and He took it away; I could forgive my friends.

> But during the night I awoke, and my first thought was how had it been possible that my friends had been so unkind, had behaved almost like enemies. Then I saw that in fact my heart was not yet free. Again I immediately confessed it to the Lord. I thought I had the victory, but the next night it came again. Is this because one does not carry the armor of God consciously during the night? Does the enemy know that when we are asleep we are not ready for battle? It is necessary that in the evening before we go to sleep our whole being and also our unconsciousness is cleansed and that we fully surrender to Him so that there is not a single starting-point left for the enemy.

> I complained about it to the Lord: "Why am I still so angry? I have experienced that You gave me grace to forgive even those who murdered my family during the war. I have always been able to preach to other people that when You tell us to love our enemies, You give us the love that You require from us. Why is there still bitterness in my heart? Lord, when I remember how often You have forgiven me in more than seventy years of my life, why is it difficult for me to forgive this? Lord, this is a problem, for I know that if I do not forgive, You will not forgive me." Then I became quiet.

That same day I heard a good illustration. When someone has been ringing the church bells—bim-bam-bim-bam—there comes the moment when he stops, no matter whether it is done electrically or by hand. But after that there often comes another bim-bam, then again a bim, then again a bam, and perhaps still a few times more. But he does not worry about that, because he knows that there has come an end to the bell-ringing, and very soon the bim-bams will stop. So it is also with the bitterness one has brought to the Lord. Bim-bams can come back, but then we must simply bring them again to the Lord. He is Victor, and soon He makes it possible by the Holy Spirit that instead of being annoyed, we love those who have sinned against us. When other people make it hard for us, then we must pray that the Lord will use this for our sanctification. Pray for them and love them as the Holy Spirit in us loves them. Then this becomes a practical training for the victory of the final battle. This experience has helped me to counsel many other people who had to resist the same temptations. I was not able to do it, but Jesus was Victor. He gave it to me. That helped them to turn their eyes in the right direction to look on high. I have learned still more. I have seen that my heart was too much tied to this work. I would not give in because my sister Betsie had inspired me to start it, for what God had told her at that time in the concentration camp had become my mission later on.

So I had to learn not to live out of the past, but to be obedient to the vocation I had to fulfill now. The Lord also sets us free from the bonds of the good past. If we will follow Jesus in all things, then we go the way of the Cross, and this includes too that very often we are not understood even by our own friends. The Lord gives grace to be able to accept fully...being misunderstood. When I get bitter feelings against my friends, then I pray to the Lord Jesus to take up my thoughts. In my imagination I have a talk with Him and my friends together. Then He gives His love and peace, and all bitterness disappears out of my heart. This experience has made me richer and stronger.[3]

A Heart Problem

* * *

Personal experiences in my own life and ministry have taught me a great deal about the importance of forgiving others from the heart. For instance, I remember one young woman who thought she only needed healing from a physical heart problem. In truth, her greatest need was to be set free from the bitterness filling her heart.

After delivering my message to an audience in Houston one evening, I requested that all those desiring prayer come forward. As I prayed with those who responded, I became aware of a young brunette who was waiting her turn for prayer. Before I reached her, I perceived that she had unforgiveness in her heart.

When I questioned her about it, She didn't answer me immediately concerning her unforgiveness. Instead, she told me of her great need. She had heart trouble and was facing surgery the next morning. She needed a miracle. She had heard that I had a miraculous healing ministry, so she had come desiring to be healed of her heart trouble.

I gently explained to her that her sin of unforgiveness stood as a barrier between her and the divine gift of healing provided for her through the atoning sacrifice of Jesus Christ. Isaiah 53:5 says:

But he was wounded for our transgressions, he was bruised for our iniquities: the

chastisement of our peace was upon him; and with his stripes we are healed.

All this young girl wanted me to do was lay my hands on her heart and pray in obedience to the Scriptures. However, I knew that my prayers wouldn't do her any good until she first forgave in obedience to God.

And be ye kind one to another, tender-hearted, *forgiving one another, even as God for Christ's sake hath forgiven you.*

Ephesians 4:32

The problem was that this young woman didn't want to forgive! But I wasn't going to pray for her until she did. I told her,"Experience has taught me through many years of ministry that unforgiveness, hatred, resentment, anger, grudges and bitterness are the biggest barriers that keep people from receiving a divine gift of healing in their bodies or in their souls."

The young woman began to tell me why it was so hard for her to forgive. She had been sexually abused by her family's physician, who was a friend of the family. This doctor's abuse had scarred her life, causing her to suffer many health problems. She had also endured a lack of good care from others in the medical profession. Up to that point, she had not forgiven any of those who had caused her to suffer mentally and physically.

I carefully explained to her that her unforgiveness could have opened the door to her heart problem. I stressed that forgiveness is a choice we make. We don't necessarily have to feel anything. We just make the decision to forgive with our whole hearts. As difficult as it may be to make that decision, God wants us to do it for our own good out of obedience to Him, because He loves us and knows that unforgiveness is like poison in our system.

After about an hour, this young woman began to see the truth. She had been in emotional bondage to her past abusers. Facing heart surgery the next morning, she realized she had to make a decision that evening. She chose to forgive them all and to let go of all her anger and bitterness.

It was a real spiritual breakthrough for her. We all rejoiced at her decision!

Finally, I laid my hands on her heart and asked God to totally heal her. It was a simple prayer, but we sensed a strong presence of the Lord.

The next morning, I was surprised by an early phone call. The young woman was calling from the hospital. Doctors took another X ray, and the results showed that her heart was totally healed!

This woman broke her covenant with unforgiveness and received a miracle. Afterwards, she went into Christian work helping young people, and all these years she has stayed free!

THE HOUSE OF FORGIVENESS

* * *

Many years ago, God blessed our family with a wonderful vacation home. I have named it "The House of Forgiveness," because it was my obedient act of forgiveness that moved God's hand in blessing us with it.

When my husband's company merged with another one, there was a couple who really gave us a bad time.

This couple perceived that there wasn't room for two executives in the new organization. The fierceness of their ensuing efforts to oust my husband from his executive position left me miserable.

At the time, I was battling cancer, and the ache in my heart was almost as painful as the ache in my body. Lies flew over our heads constantly like black ravens. Earlier we had all been friends. We had even bought property for vacation homes near each other. Of course, after the conflict began, I didn't want to be located anywhere near them.

So one day our realtor showed us a lovely lot on which we could build our dream home. *At last,* I thought, *God answered my prayer!* Unusual excitement came over me, and I almost agreed to the purchase.

However, I recognized that even though I felt excited, I wasn't sensing God's peace in my heart. My prayer had always been that we would buy the home that the Lord desired for us, so I resisted the strong impulse to purchase.

We continued to look at many places, but none were right for us. One day our family was staying at a motel near the lake when my husband and I decided to put our sons in the car and drive over to look at our site, located next to that couple's home. On the way back, I thought about the couple and said, "I forgive those people for what they did to us, but I can't forget it."

Our sons (who were young then) laughed heartily and said, "If you can't forget, you haven't forgiven!"

Those words were like arrows to my heart! My sons spoke the truth! (Forgetting an offense doesn't mean we have a memory lapse. It means the pain and poison of the memory are removed with our forgiveness.)

For two years, I had walked in self-deception. I had made a secret covenant with unforgiveness—secret even to myself. I mentally believed I had forgiven the couple, but true forgiveness had not issued forth from my heart. The spiritual transaction had not yet been made, so I was still in bondage to unforgiveness.

You see, God is a Spirit and the Father of spirits; we as His children must accordingly forgive with our *hearts*, not just with our mental processes.

When I returned home, I knelt before the Lord, broke my covenant with unforgiveness and truly forgave the couple from my heart.

The next time we went to our property on the lake, the woman walked over to visit and invited me into her house. As I crossed the couple's threshold, I received a miracle. In my heart I felt the tangible love of God for them! (Rom. 5:5.) To my surprise, each beat of my heart seemed to say, "I love you! I love you!"

We are told to love our enemies. As we choose to obey this commandment, we find that He supplies us with *His* love.

After that remarkable experience, my husband and I returned to our motel and found a note from our realtor requesting that we call him about a house he thought we would like. We did, and the realtor took us to a house that fulfilled every desire of our hearts. This home was already decorated with my favorite colors, and every room had a lake view, just as my husband had desired!

We bought this dream home—our House of Forgiveness—and have enjoyed it ever since. For two years, I had prayed diligently for this home, and my prayers didn't seem to be answered. But when I forgave with my whole heart, my petition was granted immediately.

The barrier had been with me, *not* God. For two years, I thought I was waiting on the Lord. But the truth was, He had actually been waiting on me!

MAN'S WAR—GOD'S LOVE

* * *

Just how great is the power of God's love and forgiveness? I read an amazing story from the annals of World War II that gives us a little more insight into that question.

Those Americans who are too young to remember World War II should at least be familiar with the date December 7, 1941, a day President Franklin D. Roosevelt said would live in infamy. On this day, Japan attacked the American military base in Pearl Harbor, Hawaii.

Americans awoke on the morning of December 8 to startling news: The United States had declared war on Japan. Life on planet earth would never be the same again. The *World Book Encyclopedia* states that World War II was the mightiest struggle that mankind had ever seen.[4]

In their book *Soldiers of the Sun,* Merion and Susie Harries relate some of the documented atrocities that the Japanese military were guilty of committing during this tragic war:

> The atrocities committed by the Imperial Japanese Army are impossible to catalog. The number and the hideous variety of the crimes defy even the most twisted

imagination: murder on a scale amounting to genocide; rapes beyond counting; vivisection; cannibalism; torture; American prisoners of war allowed to drown in excrement in the "hell ships" taking them back to Japan for use as forced labor; civilian prisoners used as human sandbags during air raids; Burmese coolies, dead and dying, stuffed under the sleeping platforms of other laborers on the Burma-Siam Railway....

...In the Philippines, three civilians were caught escaping from an internment camp and sentenced to death. The firing party used automatic pistols, but the three men were not killed outright.... Even in their grave the men were still moaning and groaning, but the Japanese officer in charge ordered the Filipino gravediggers, on pain of death, to fill it in. "On Guadalcanal," reported a Japanese private dispassionately in his diary, "two prisoners were dissected while still alive...and their livers were taken out."[5]

Japan's bitter war against the other nations of Asia resulted in women being conscripted as sex slaves to the Imperial Army.

Meanwhile, allied forces continued to invade strategic Japanese territory. Terror struck again in March, 1945, when air raids destroyed parts of Tokyo.

Finally, the U.S. Decided to use the recently developed atomic bomb in order to end the long, bloody war. On August 6, 1945, the U.S. dropped the bomb on Hiroshima. Three days later, another bomb wiped out approximately two square miles in Nagasaki. It was reported that more than 200,000 people were either killed or wounded in these two attacks.

The devastation to the Japanese people was unbelievable. The effects of atomic radiation resulted in untold numbers of burns, diseases and death.

Events occurred rapidly after the bombs were dropped. It was obvious to Japanese leaders that Japan had lost the war. On August 14, 1945, Emperor Hirohito announced that Japan had agreed to end the war. Allied military occupation began in late August, with General Douglas MacArthur named Allied Commander.

Under General MacArthur's orders, the Allies tried twenty-eight major Japanese leaders for war crimes. "Before Pearl Harbor it was not regarded as possible to attribute responsibility for acts of war to specific individuals, nor was aggressive war seen as a crime under international law," write Merion and Susie Harries.[6]

The International Military Tribunal for the Far East held a trial in Tokyo. Many Japanese men were eventually convicted by the International War Crimes Tribunal, and they were held under tight security at the Sugamo Prison near Tokyo.

However, God had a plan for these condemned men, as well as a person to implement His plan. She was an elderly missionary.

Irene Webster-Smith, called "Sensei" in Japan, had gone to Japan as a young Irish girl to serve her Savior, the Lord Jesus Christ. She had established Sunshine Home, taking in unwanted and sick babies to nurse them back to health and raise them in a Christian home. She called the children her little "Sunbeams."

This post-World War II story of God's love begins with Sensei at an age when most people are enjoying retirement. Noshi San, a former little Sunbeam, had married a widower with four children, and they lived in a small town outside of Tokyo. Noshi San had recently started a Sunday school in her own home. She wrote to Sensei, hoping that Sensei would come and speak to these women.

Sensei agreed to visit the Sunday school class. After she spoke to the group, one of the women introduced herself to Sensei:

"I am the wife of Nishizawa San," she said.

Sensei felt a moment of shock. She knew, as did everyone else in Japan, that Nishizawa San was one of the military leaders convicted of war crimes and held in Sugamo Prison, condemned to death.

"I know the Savior myself," Mrs. Nishizawa said, "but I am deeply concerned about my husband; I want very much for him to become a Christian before he dies."[7]

She begged Sensei to go see him. She even volunteered to give up her visiting privileges of a half hour each month to Sensei.

Sensei could not refuse. She knew it would not be easy to get permission.... But difficulties had never stopped Sensei yet, and she was not about to let them now....

At last the American officer said: "We have decided that since this man is entitled to one clemency interview, we will let you see him, *providing* this is his choice. We must ask him first if he wants to see you."

Sensei bowed her thanks and went home to wait.

Some days later she was notified that Nishizawa would see her.[8]

At the grim prison, Sensei was led to the interview booth. She referred to the booklet on the gospel of John that Nishizawa's wife had left with him. Sensei told Nishizawa that Christ had died for all mankind and offered to forgive anyone of anything if he truly repented from his heart. She also explained to the prisoner about his eternal soul.

Nishizawa listened intently. He asked Sensei:

"Do you mean He could forgive *my* sins? ...I have committed terrible sins."

Sensei said firmly, "...In the blood of Jesus Christ there is cleansing for *all* sin."

"What must I do to get this forgiveness?" he asked.

"Believe in the Lord Jesus Christ and thou shall be saved," Sensei said.

Nishizawa repeated the words of salvation. Sensei began to read from John 14: "'Let not your heart be troubled...'" for she knew that Nishizawa was soon to die.[9]

Nishizawa confessed that Jesus Christ had saved him that day. Before exiting the prison, Sensei left him with this challenge:

"I want you to find...one person in the prison and tell him what the Lord has done for you. Will you do that?"

"How can I?" he said. "I am in solitary confinement."

"There is some way," Sensei said with conviction.[10]

Sensei returned to Nishizawa's wife to tell her of her husband's conversion. Soon after that, Sensei was called back to the Sugamo Prison. A war criminal named Shibano had requested a clemency interview with her.

Sensei's old face lighted with joy. She knew that Nishizawa had brought a soul to Christ....

One by one the prisoners passed the word on—their witness of what Jesus Christ had done for them, and now meant to them—and one by one they asked for clemency interviews with Sensei. She provided Testaments for all of the war criminals, and she prayed for them.

In all, fourteen of the war criminals accepted Christ
through her. Thirteen of them later asked for baptism, and
the rite was performed by a Baptist prison chaplain.[11]

Each war criminal felt unworthy of forgiveness
because of his multiple murderous acts. Sensei was sent
by Almighty God to give these men the truth about His
forgiving love—forgiveness made possible only by the
shed blood of His Son. Jesus had provided a way of
pardon for them.

As the prisoners received this truth, their covenant
with eternal doom was broken, for it is God's truth that
sets men free when they receive Jesus into their eternal
spirits. *God's* way is the *love* way.

The men were no longer warlords; they were new
creatures in Christ. His love had set them free!

Sensei, God's general, went to visit and comfort the
families of the converted men. Even the military police-
men asked Sensei to talk to them about Jesus Christ. And
when it was time for the Japanese warlords to be
executed, they died triumphantly, with their Bibles in
their hands and singing "Nearer, My God, to Thee."[12]
Meanwhile, the other prisoners who were left behind
sang, "God Be With You Till We Meet Again."[13]

**Though your sins be as scarlet, they
shall be as white as snow; though they be
red like crimson, they shall be as wool.**

Isaiah 1:18

This account of Sensei and the warlords demonstrates just how unfathomable the power of God's love
and forgiveness is. Even more unfathomable is the truth
that His love and power to forgive reside on the inside of

us. Because His love has been shed abroad in our hearts and we no longer need to make covenants with bitterness, resentment and the like, we can forgive others just as He has forgiven us!

8

THE DOMINO EFFECT

Agreeing with the devil's lies brings dangerous consequences—not just in one person's life but in many others' as well. I call this the domino effect.

The following testimony from a dedicated Christian woman named Mary Jean Warlen and her daughter Susie touched my heart so deeply. It also provides great insight into the domino effect that one casualty covenant can have on many lives. I present these two women's stories, beginning with Susie's, in all the love with which they shared it with me.

AN UNEXPECTED GOODBYE
• • •

Our story begins when a family—three brothers and a nephew—left Sweden in 1878, changing their name from Anderson to Warlen while still on the boat to America. The young men's choice of a new name was significant. They were embarking on a journey to start a new life with a new name that in Swedish translates as "our land."

A covenant trust with the land began with their adoption of that name. They settled in Kansas and became wheat farmers, teaching their children a diligent work ethic to be passed on to future generations.

One of the brothers, Millen Warlen, had a grandson born during the Great Depression on March 1, 1931, to Wesley and Thelma Gordon Warlen. This grandson was my daddy—Wesley M. Warlen Jr.

Now we move ahead fifty-eight years to May 14, 1989, Mother's Day. My mom called to tell me that Dad was not feeling well. That surprised me because he was never sick. But I was not able to talk to him because the pastor and one of the elders were partaking of Communion with him.

My dad was an elder at his church and enjoyed leading worship for the congregation. It was very unusual for him not to attend a church service. I lived 600 miles away from Mom and Dad. But my faith was strong, and I knew God could do anything. So I went on to my own church to pray for him.

During the service, some dear friends joined with me at the altar to pray for my dad. I had the greatest confidence that God heard my prayer and would answer the cry of my heart. From my parents I had learned the truth of 1 John 5:14-15:

> **And this is the confidence that we have in him, that, if we ask any thing according to his will, he heareth us: And if we know that he hear us, whatsoever we ask, we know that we have the petitions that we desired of him.**

I had no doubts, because my faith was strong. My day continued free from worry until my mom called that evening and said, "We are taking Dad to the hospital. It's his heart."

I immediately packed a bag and jumped in the car with my roommate to drive home. My faith was still strong, but I could sense fear entering my heart. As we drove, I began to think about what might happen, but the possibility of Dad's dying never entered my mind.

It was a ten-hour drive. Three hours down the road, we stopped to call the hospital to see how my dad was doing. But after several futile attempts to find a family member to talk to, I finally called home.

My sister answered the phone and immediately gave it to my mom without sharing a word. I asked Mom, "How's Daddy?"

"Your daddy is gone," Mom said quietly.

All I remember after hearing those shocking words is yelling back in the telephone, "*No!* He *can't* be dead!"

But Dad *was* gone. My roommate helped me back in the car and took over the driving, holding my hand as I cried the rest of the way home.

For the first time in my life, my faith was shaken, because I knew that with God, all things are possible. So why did my dad die?

This was the beginning of the hardening of my heart. After Dad's funeral, I began a pattern of busyness so I wouldn't have to deal with any of my feelings.

As the years went by, the busyness grew. So did the pain, because I never forgave God for taking my daddy. The day came when, through a series of remarkable circumstances, I finally had to deal honestly with all the hurts that had built up in my heart over the years.

I realized that I was mad at God. It was hard for me to imagine that I had continued to serve God after my dad's death, thinking that I loved the same God I accused of taking my daddy. I had even been very effective in ministry. But the reality was that deep in my heart *I was mad at Him.*

I asked God's forgiveness for blaming Him for all the disappointments in my life. However, I still didn't know what to do about the mystery that had plagued me for years. *I just couldn't understand why my daddy died.* It didn't make sense.

Then God led me to someone who would help me understand—Mickie Winborn. God knew that my repentance was real and that my heart was ready to be healed of the hurts. I was ready to deal with the truth, no matter what it was.

Mickie and I began talking. She asked me more in-depth questions about my dad's death than most people had ever thought to ask. Then she said to me, "*You just didn't understand.*"

That's when I knew God had appointed our time together. She began to explain casualty covenants to me and gave me her book *Through a Glass, Darkly.*

As I read her book, God began to soften my heart. I was finally beginning to understand.

About that time, my mother and I dicussed what actually happened that day—something I never knew. My mother had taken my dad to the hospital. As Dad lay on the emergency room table, the doctor asked him if his father had died of a heart attack. Dad had sadly nodded his head yes as tears filled his eyes.

When I heard this, I realized that my father had accepted a casualty with death at that moment. I could even understand how it had happened. For the past nine years since Dad's death, every time the date of May 14 came up in conversation, my only thought had been that it was the day my daddy had died.

So I know when the doctor asked my dad about his father, Dad realized that it was the same day *his* daddy had died sixteen years earlier. No doubt Satan told him he would die of a heart attack, just as his father had. I believe that Dad just accepted a covenant with death, thinking it was his time to go as well.

So I finally understood. God didn't take my daddy! *I had blamed God for what Satan had done!* My dad had been deceived by Satan into believing that he would die from heart failure because his own dad died on the same date, May 14, due to heart problems.

That night I prayed, breaking any casualty covenants I had ever made in my whole life regarding my family or myself. I felt a release in my heart and a new love for God, my Father. I was able to share this spiritual principle with my mother and my younger brother. When my brother heard the explanation of the casualty covenant, he broke the curse on our family of dying young from heart attacks.

After sharing what I had learned with my mother, I heard words of truth from her heart about Dad's dying moments that I had never been able to even address or discuss during those past nine years of my own personal grieving time. During a three-way phone call with Mickie Winborn and my mother, I began to understand even more as my mom related her part of this family story.

FROM MOM'S PERSPECTIVE
• • •

Susie's mother shared with me that Wesley M. Warlen and she, Mary Jean Payne, had established their marriage covenant on May 12, 1961, declaring before the throne of grace in their vows that they would be one until death parted them. On their twenty-eighth anniversary, they chose to celebrate with a lovely Christian gathering of friends around the Communion table. That night, Wesley was honored for his integrity and loving nature by this wonderful Christian community of believers.

Mary Jean went on to share:

Wes and I were quiet and reflective as we drove home through the peaceful Kentucky countryside on this twelfth day of May in 1989, our anniversary. We were remembering the beauties and joys of the past years as a Christian family. We felt just a bit lonely for days gone by when the children were all at home, yet hopeful for a future of growing old together (although we had only discussed that subject once).

The following day was Saturday. We spent most of the day apart, doing our own outreach activities. Yet at sundown, my heart began to alert me to rush home to my husband. My friend and I had been going from church to church, distributing literature and praying with people in our community on a worthwhile project. But as we were parting, I unexpectedly began to weep as I thought of the love of my remarkable husband.

It is a shame that we often don't recognize the magnitude of impending events. We need to be sharpened to know when God is prompting us to understand things more deeply and to be more aware of situations in our lives so we don't miss something important.

My friend and I prayed for my husband, whom she, too, loved deeply—as one would love an elder brother or mentor.

That evening, Wes began to experience some slight muscle pains in his chest. Our wonderful family friends who were also doctors lived right next door, and they suggested some medication to relieve the symptoms. If that didn't help him, they told us we should call them for further assistance.

On Sunday morning at breakfast we were planning to celebrate Mother's Day. But to my surprise, I found myself suggesting to the rest of the family, "Let's celebrate Father's Day today instead. Then in June, we can celebrate Mother's Day"—not realizing that Wes wouldn't be with us for any further celebrations.

Another clue went unnoticed: Our pastor and one of Wes' fellow elders came to pray for him, their brother in the Lord, before church. What a glorious time they had sharing together and reminiscing about the victories they had shared in the Lord Jesus Christ! We had all participated in these victories during the birthing and establishing of our church, which was founded on intercessory prayer and on reaching the nations through prayer.

I went on to church. Now as I look back and ponder the events of that morning, I wonder what it was like for Wes.

He spent the afternoon quietly as the young people came by to share their walk with the Lord Jesus Christ.

Our daughter Patti was due home from college, but she meandered the whole day, arriving shortly before we took her dad to the hospital. Matthew, our youngest son, was in and out during the day.

We spoke about Dad's not feeling well with our oldest son, Michael, who lived nearby in Nashville, Tennessee. The only one who didn't have the opportunity to speak to Wes was our daughter Susie, who lived 600 miles away. That missed opportunity to hear her daddy's voice proved to be devastating to Susie personally.

My own precious dad came by to visit Wes in his freshly refurbished red truck. Wesley had happily helped my dad with that truck the day before, as well as helping him build new rooms in our church.

The whole family was alerted, and most were assembled. Yet none of us were prepared for the events that followed. We took Wes to the hospital with pains in his chest and arm, and the drama began to unfold.

Now, we had moved to this small farming community in the first place as a result of a prayer covenant with the Lord Jesus Christ. Wes had accepted a new job, believing it would not only be beneficial for him, but that this move would be a blessing for all six of us. Over the years, we had made many precious friends who did prove to be a great blessing to us when this crisis arose.

Because of the special love that the community had for my husband, the phone alert went out that something was wrong with their wonderful brother in the Lord. The director of the hospital, a close personal friend, called the pastor and the other church elders.

Friends of fifteen years began to arrive to stand in prayer and minister love to our son and daughter Matthew and Patti. The Christian manager of our company and his wife stood right with us, praying for God's protection during those next hours.

The head nurse was a wonderful, caring friend and a member of our congregation. The assisting nurse was the mother of a young lady who had been on Wes' softball team. He had coached for several years, and he and the mother had developed a close friendship.

Our neighbors, who were the attending doctors (both husband and wife), arrived during this critical time, addressing the medical emergency as it developed. In the emergency room, I stood by Wes' side at the place of prayer, watching the events unfold that would change our lives so drastically.

The doctors took an EKG, revealing that Wes' heart was okay and he was not having a heart attack. Afterwards, the attending emergency doctor, whom I didn't know, came to ask Wes about the medical history of his family.

This scene is frozen in my mind, and the following narration will help take you there with me.

The doctor said, "Mr. Warlen, tell me about the medical history of your father. I see that he, too, died of a heart condition."

At that moment, I watched my husband's eyes fill with tears. It was so unlike him to cry, and I immediately put my hand on his shoulder and said, "Wes, your dad died of a heart condition due to his having scarlet fever as a child."

It was at that moment that I lost touch with the thoughts of my husband. He was now focused on the death of his own father, who had died on May 14, 1973.

A Crisis Unfolds
* * *

Now events began to quickly unfold. (The pain of reliving this story is bearable now because God has revealed the truth and is setting our family free.)

I leaned over to kiss my beloved husband. I told him to call on the name of Jesus and pray in his prayer language, which he immediately began to do. Doctors declared a medical alert in the emergency room. I stood by quietly because I didn't want the medical staff to tell me to leave. Our pastor was standing against the wall, looking at me with concern.

The staff was on alert mode. The head nurse put her hand on my shoulder with such pressure that it startled me. She looked deep into my eyes and whispered, *"Pray!"* with such intensity that I almost lost my breath. After they administered a strong dose of medication to Wes, his blood pressure dramatically dropped. Our doctor neighbors arrived just as an ambulance was called to transfer Wes to a larger hospital in a nearby town.

Wes' eyes never left mine as the medical staff wheeled him away. That was the moment our lives changed forever.

We followed the ambulance, the manager and his wife taking Patti and me in their car. Our son Matthew rode with our neighbor, while his doctor wife rode in the ambulance with Wesley.

As the ambulance sped into the night, the siren calling out in the dark, my heart began to race into intercession. On the way to the town where the larger hospital was located, we saw an ambulance returning through the town, headed for the hospital we had just left. We didn't know my beloved husband was in that ambulance, so we kept going.

If this crisis had happened nine years later, the convenience of car phones would have kept us from driving on to another town, not knowing that they had taken Wes back to die at our small hospital in the town where we had lovingly raised our children for fifteen years. When I finally returned to that little hospital, I was told those cold words, "He didn't make it."

I misunderstood. Somehow thinking the doctor said Wes *had* made it, I shouted, "Hallelujah!" I later understood my spontaneous outburst to be an unwitting victory cry because Wes was now in the presence of the Lord.

A calm settled over all the family and friends gathered at the hospital as the truth of Wes' death sunk in. The medical staff left me alone to visit my beautiful husband of twenty-eight years. I looked at him lying there so peacefully and thought about all the questions for which I had no answers. I pondered, *How could this have happened? I just don't understand why.*

As I joined two of our four children in the waiting room among our loving, caring friends, I asked if we could all join hands and sing "He Is Lord."[1] Those moments are etched forever in our hearts. The words to this song are so true: "Every knee shall bow, every tongue confess that Jesus Christ is Lord."

The thought of dying on the same day his own father had died sixteen years earlier must have entered into Wes' mind in the twinkling of an eye. Death is lurking at every corner, and we need to be wise to the wiles of the enemy's camp.

Living in a small country town, we felt at liberty to go to the funeral home to pray. I wanted to ask the Lord to raise Wes from the dead. Years earlier, Smith Wigglesworth had done the same not many miles from where we lived. Also, a man whom God had healed miraculously of a massive head injury was speaking in a nearby town. We called this man, asking him to come.

At the funeral home, as I rolled the casket containing my husband's body into the parlor, my faith was in full measure, supported by believing friends and our pastor.

However, as we prayed with all our hearts for an extended period of time, I sensed the Father God whisper to my heart, *You've done all you can do; he's Mine.* So I released my husband to the Lord with blessing. In great brokenness, I went home to help reach out to four broken hearts—our children's. I wanted just to hold them and cry for a season.

THE MANY FACES OF GRIEF
· · ·

The underlying factor for all of us who were involved with this drama—family, friends and coworkers—was the burning question: *Why did it happen?* We all kept saying, "I just don't understand why!"

Incidentally, Proverbs 3:5-6 was etched in the first concrete step of our lovely country home:

> **Trust in the Lord with all thine heart;**
> **and lean not unto thine own understanding.**
> **In all thy ways acknowledge him, and he**
> **shall direct thy paths.**

For all the years we lived in that home, we had written that Scripture in our hearts. The entire Warlen family had memorized it. Yet here we were in a situation that defied human understanding—that is, until the words *casualty covenants* entered our lives.

Now, each of the four children are believers, yet the responses to their daddy's death had an impact on their own responses to life. Anger at God flooded Susie's heart to the degree that the next nine years were filled with great activity to cover up the pain. Of course, Susie had never heard my account of what had happened in the emergency room until we made a three-way phone call with Mickie Winborn. Up until then, we'd had too much hurt to walk through the sequence of events together.

Another of my adult children became so family-oriented that we made constant adjustments in an effort to keep us functioning as a family. However, due to our scattering to various locations, it became an impossible and unrealistic endeavor—no matter how hard one tried.

Another chose denial and became somewhat indifferent to life, losing any real, focused purpose and letting others take charge.

The fourth of my children became so aware of health needs that fear of other family-related diseases became a

163

great focus: *Great-grandmother died of it; Grandmother died of it; therefore, I am going to get it too!* Evidently those diseases weren't necessarily hereditary but could have come as a result of casualty covenants.

These are subtle thoughts that rob people of the joy of living an abundant life in Christ. Fear is transferable to others and surfaces in different ways. Eventually it becomes perpetual, attracting adverse situations that need not harass one who wants to be strong in the Lord.

Nine years after Wes' death, our family at last began to find some answers to our questions about his sudden and sad death.

I called the head nurse over the emergency room that night to share with her how Susie, in her own brokenness, might have stumbled into some answers to hard questions. This wonderful nurse had become a casualty herself as the result of my husband's death, leaving nursing as a result of the situation.

As this precious friend spent the last moments of my husband's life in the ambulance with him, she heard him crying out to Jesus to help him with the pain. The main thing she recalls is how he received grace in his time of great need. Still, all she could say afterwards was, *"I just don't understand."* She had seen death before, and she knew Wes' death didn't need to happen.

As I explained to my friend the reason for writing this story, she remembered the tears in Wesley's eyes as he lay in the emergency room. She also knew that this wasn't in character for him. At that time, the fatal dose of medication had not yet been administered. As she listened to me explain about casualty covenants, she realized that it was a valid explanation to most puzzling events—events that changed even the course of *her* life.

Much good has come forth since Wes' death as each of us has chosen to walk in faith, run hard after God and not let grief overtake us. Yet we still needed answers to the questions that burned in our hearts for so long.

Sometimes difficult situations occur in all our lives that sharpen us by the Holy Spirit, making us alert and helping us walk more circumspectly through them. If we deal with these trials according to God's Word, we will see His goodness, rather than a whole domino effect of casualties coming forth in our lives.

That is the purpose of sharing our family story.

And the purpose of my heart is also to alert others of the possibility of a domino effect so they will stand firm on the Word and not let the enemy needlessly rob, kill or destroy. God is sovereign, and His wisdom is precious and worth digging for. As believers seek Him in His Word and by His Spirit, He will help them walk through the trial and find answers to the difficult questions in their hearts.

As I ponder these thoughts in my heart, my faith is strengthened and my resolve to serve a living God with all my heart is greater than ever before.

ANOTHER CHALLENGE
* * *

Since our family learned about casualty covenants, we have had other situations in which we've had to make choices about whether we would agree with the enemy or Almighty God.

For instance, one time I was getting ready to leave within two hours for an international trip. One of my daughters was with me. Suddenly we got an emergency phone call with the dreaded message that my other daughter had a lump in her breast.

It was an extremely serious situation, and she needed immediate surgical attention. Leaping to my feet, I declared, *"No!"* I was speaking to this assignment of death that was trying to invade the purpose of God once again. I shared with the daughter facing surgery that on my side of the family, noncancerous fibroid tumors had been found on several occasions but all had been benign.

Our family's focus had been on the casualty covenants made on my husband's side of the family. Now the enemy was trying to set up a casualty covenant on my side of the family. I loudly declared, "No, no, *no!* No more! This is enough!"

I returned home from overseas after being delayed four days and missing my daughter's exploratory surgery. The diagnosis after the surgery was that the growth was only a benign infectious mastoiditis and nothing more.

Had fear gripped our hearts and had we not let wisdom rule our minds, we might have brought forth a casualty covenant. But out of our own mouths came the victory shout, "No more, Satan—*no more!*"

A TESTIMONY TO BLESS THE WORLD
• • •

My family is still in the process of growing, and I am still sharing these truths with my children. I am watching the enemy release his hold on situations, and we are celebrating more and more victories. We will keep declaring that "He Is Lord," just as we sang on May 14, 1989, gathering in a circle of love with friends in Christ. We will also keep sharing this story of victory.

I know that I am personally set free in a greater way because of what I now know about casualty covenants. At Wes' funeral, a prophetic word was spoken that Wes Warlen's testimony would go around the world. Since I am involved with International Prayer Outreach, I thought it was part of my responsibility to talk about Wes' life wherever I went. But now, this clarity of truth in regard to Wes' death will truly be a testimony as it is shared around the earth.

In this hour, we must become wise to the danger of casualty covenants and particularly of the devastation of the domino effect one person's casualty covenant can have on so many others. Only then can we live free from the trap laid by the enemy to ensnare us and our loved ones in casualty covenants.

9

GUIDELINES FOR
GODLY DECISIONS
AND GOOD SUCCESS

Since choices determine our destinies, the devil is determined to use casualty covenants to distract us from making decisions that ultimately bring peace and joy. Therefore, we must align our minds with the mind of God—who loves us and knows the best for us—in order to make godly decisions and enjoy success in life.

GUIDELINES FOR GUIDANCE

The following are guidelines that will help you escape pitfalls and make successful decisions for your life so you can avoid becoming a casualty.

1. Gather all the available facts and study them. (Prov. 18:13.)

2. Ask God for His knowledge of hidden factors. (Luke 8:17.)

3. Ask God with thanksgiving for His wisdom on the matter. (Prov. 2:3-10; 8:20,21; James 1:5-8; 3:14-18.)

4. Do not make a hasty decision. (Prov. 11:14; 19:2.)

5. Make decisions that maintain peace in your heart, not necessarily in your head. (Col. 3:15.)

6. Ask God for specific, related Scriptures (a *rhema* word—that is, a sentence or a phrase "quickened," or made alive, to you for the moment about your situation) on the matter. (Acts 17:2; Luke 24:32.) His words to you will never violate His principles or His nature.

7. Make sure the circumstances of your life are favorable. (Prov. 16:7-9; 20:24.)

These seven points presuppose five things:

• That you have received Jesus Christ as your Savior.

• That you are not knowingly sinning.

• That you desire to please God.

• That you have knowledge of God's Word.

• That you regularly study the Scriptures.

Besides the seven guidelines above and the five points listed, it is important to know that receiving guidance from God often comes in the form of an inner impression in the intuition of your spirit.

The revelation in the believer's spirit is more reliable than the thoughts in his head. God's guidance is never confused or compulsory. It is not vague, but it does require time for the brain to prove that the guidance received is truly from the Holy Spirit. One of the principles of God's operation is that we use our intelligence and cooperate with Him.

Therefore, a passive mind which waits for an external force to activate it offers an invitation for deception by evil spirits and is contrary to God's Word: **Wherefore be ye not unwise, but *understanding* what the will of the Lord is** (Eph. 5:17).

Also, the Holy Spirit may lead you to seek counsel from godly leaders: **Not forsaking the assembling of ourselves together...** (Heb. 10:25).[1]

The book of Joshua specifically states a principle for success:

> **This book of the law shall not depart out of thy mouth; but thou shalt meditate therein day and night, that thou mayest observe to do according to all that is written therein: for then thou shalt make thy way prosperous, and then thou shalt have good success.**
>
> **Joshua 1:8**

When circumstances appear unfavorable, you can pray to God to change the circumstances. (Circumstances can change, but God never changes.) If the circumstances do not change after a reasonable period of time spent waiting on God, then the matter should be postponed until all three of the pertinent guidelines for a godly decision are operating simultaneously.

Bob Mumford explains more about these three beacon-light guidelines in his book *Take Another Look at Guidance:*

Three Harbor Lights—
Navigation in the Spirit
by Bob Mumford

Prior to electronic navigation, a certain harbor in Italy could only be reached by sailing up a narrow channel between dangerous rocks and shoals. Over the years, many ships have been wrecked there, and navigation is extremely hazardous.

To guide the ships safely into port, three lights have been mounted on three huge poles in the harbor. When the three lights are perfectly lined up and seen as one, the ship can safely turn to begin navigation up the narrow channel. If the pilot sees two or three lights separately, he knows that he is off course and in danger! He must continue to maneuver his vessel until the lights perfectly line up before he can safely turn into the harbor.

For our safety in navigating our ship of life God has provided three beacons to guide us. The same rules of navigation apply to us as to the harbor pilot. The three lights must be perfectly lined up as one before it is safe for us to proceed up the channel. The three harbor lights of guidance are:

1. The Word of God (objective standard)
2. The Holy Spirit (subjective witness)
3. Circumstances (divine providence)[2]

At times, there is an intuitive "knowing" that God gives to His people that combines the above three principles. This knowing is a settled sense within your spirit. The word of knowledge—a gift of the Holy Spirit—communicates it to your understanding.

You see, God is a Spirit (John 4:24), and He communicates with our spirits. One Christian I know said guidance by the Holy Spirit "...is knowing in your 'knower'!"

Once you have fulfilled all the above guidelines with prayer and thanksgiving, it is then time to relinquish all to God without anxiety, staying prayerfully alert on the matter.

Finally, let me share an observation on receiving God's guidance through prayer. It comes from an unknown author:

If the wish is not right, God answers NO.

If the time is not right, God answers SLOW.

If I am not right, God answers GROW.

If everything is right, God answers GO!

FLEECES AREN'T ALWAYS AS WHITE AS SNOW
. . .

It is such a temptation to ask God to confirm His will for us by giving us an outward sign, or a "fleece." Unfortunately, it is very possible to receive confirmations from outward signs that are contrary to God's will.

I saw a dramatic example of this years ago when the use of drugs first hit our neighborhood schools. I gathered teachers, school nurses and mothers into my home and invited speakers to come and explain to us the subject of teenage drug addiction. Those at the gathering shared this information with others, alerting our area to what had before been hidden from us.

Then a very wealthy, socially prominent woman called me, asking to hold a similar meeting in her palatial home. I agreed that this would be a great event for her to host because it would help many understand more about drug addiction.

The woman insisted that I be in charge of the entire affair. She offered to cover all expenses and open her home for the event. She wanted to fly in such people as David Wilkerson of Teen Challenge and others who had firsthand knowledge of this subject.

I hesitated to accept her offer because I knew the kind of time and effort these types of meetings require.

However, in anticipation that Jesus would be lifted up as the deliverer from drugs, I agreed.

Amazingly, whenever I spoke to other Christian leaders about this prospective meeting, they were most agreeable to participate. At a prayer meeting, one woman even said she would personally speak to David Wilkerson.

Seeing others so enthusiastic was an encouragement to me. Plans were proceeding quite well.

However, there was a problem: I felt uneasy in my spirit. All outward signs were on *go*, but all inward signs were on *no*. I had agreed to manage this function before I had consulted God. It had seemed like such a good idea! Little did I realize that I had agreed with the evil one, who was going to have a laugh at my expense.

Then I had two dreams conveying the same thought. One night I dreamed I was in an embarrassing situation. The next night, I dreamed I was in a humiliating situation.

The dreams disturbed me. Essentially, every time I had put out a fleece to see if this gathering was okay with God, I had received affirmation. But my spirit was not at peace about it, and now I'd had two distressing dreams.

Alarmed and unsettled about the anti-drug meeting we were planning, I decided to attend a special function in Dallas where I knew Reverend Kenneth E. Hagin would be speaking. I thought Reverend Hagin might share something that would help me.

At the Dallas meeting, Brother Hagin taught on exactly what I needed to hear. He explained that in the Old Testament, it was all right to put out a fleece to confirm God's will.

Reverend Hagin referred to an example of this in the book of Judges, where God told Gideon that he was to be His chosen instrument in delivering Israel from the hand of Midian. (Judg. 6:12-16.) In response, Gideon put out a fleece of wool on the threshing floor in order to test God's spoken word to him.

Then Gideon said to God, "Do not let Thine anger burn against me that I may speak once more; please let me make a test once more with the fleece, let it now be dry only on the fleece, and let there be dew on all the ground."

And God did so that night; for it was dry only on the fleece, and dew was on all the ground.

Judges 6:39,40 NAS

"However," Reverend Hagin continued, "putting out a fleece is not a valid action for today's believer, because he is under a better covenant."

Brother Hagin went on to explain that as New Testament believers, we are led by the Holy Spirit, who dwells within our spirits. In the Old Testament, God's people didn't have the Holy Spirit dwelling within them, although He was still with them.

That's why God answered Gideon by confirming the fleece experiment.

But in this age of grace, we are to be led by the Holy Spirit, not by human reasoning or fleeces. Today we have God's written Word and the inward witness of peace in our spirits to guide us.

It is dangerous to put out fleeces today because Satan can give us outward signs as false confirmation. He seeks to fleece us!

This is exactly what he did to me. His intent was to make a fool out of me and destroy my credibility in the city where we were to hold the meetings. However, the faithful Father God warned me with two dreams and unrest in my spirit.

As I listened again to Reverend Hagin's message on tape, I immediately knew that the planned gathering in the wealthy woman's home was a mistake.

As soon as I returned home from Dallas, that inner knowing was confirmed. A phone message from the woman was waiting for me. After a few preliminaries, she said that she had to call off the whole planned event because she wanted to take a trip with her husband. (I have wondered if her teenage son objected to our concerned effort to uncover drug use in our neighboring high schools, causing her to make the sudden decision to leave town.)

Thank God, I hadn't contacted any speakers for the occasion. However, I *had* contacted friends, asking them to help as volunteers to put the large meeting together. But although it *was* embarrassing to call my friends and cancel plans, the outcome wasn't nearly as bad as the devil had planned for me. I was almost fleeced by fleeces!

So don't follow the fleece—follow God instead!

Relinquishing Your Plans to God in Prayer

• • •

Let me give you another illustration of how making godly decisions—instead of covenanting with Satan's lies—brings about ultimate success.

I was ministering in California. But it seemed like nothing was working! My plans just would not move ahead. I couldn't understand the delay in developing my desires. Certainly they were simple enough.

You see, I had agreed to lead a workshop for the National Convocation of Christian Leaders at the University of San Diego in California. I had prayerfully prepared my material for the workshop and was looking forward to seeing friends there.

The convocation would last four days, and then I would be free for the weekend. While in San Diego, I wanted very much to see the famous San Diego Zoo and visit La Jolla on the Pacific Ocean.

So while I was still home in Texas, I called my friend Beverly, a member of the Convocation, hoping we could share a dormitory room and then spend a few days sightseeing together after the meetings. Beverly's phone rang and rang, but there was no answer. The time to depart for California was at hand, but all my plans were on hold.

Slowly it dawned on me—my plans were not God's plans. I came to understand that I had to let go of my holiday desires.

After some reflection, I realized that my deepest heart's desire is to serve the Lord Jesus Christ. So that made it easy to relinquish my earthly desires for His heavenly purposes. In His grace, I knelt down and surrendered my heart and plans to Him.

I had experienced a similar moment many years before when I was dying of terminal cancer—a moment in which I had relinquished my life to God, whether to life or death. Therefore, I understood the principle of the prayer of relinquishment. However, in this case, my holiday plans hadn't seemed important enough to require prayer.

Immediately after my prayer of surrender and relinquishment, Beverly called, suggesting that we share a dorm room. Once I removed the impediment of *my* will, God began to move!

A few days into the meetings, Beverly phoned her friend Lynne in nearby Encinitas. Observing Beverly's look of concern as she talked to Lynne, I knew bad news was on the line.

During the conversation, Beverly turned to me and said, "Mickie, Lynne's daughter-in-law has just received the results of an X ray. She has breast cancer." After a hurried consultation, we agreed to visit Lynne and her family at the conclusion of our meetings.

My workshop went well, and it was well attended. At the last meeting of the convocation, I was asked to lead the prayer.

Generally, I wear subdued clothing at such meetings so as to blend with the other leaders in their conservative suits. However, Beverly and I planned to leave San Diego as soon as the meeting was over. We wouldn't have time enough to change, so I was dressed to depart, wearing brightly colored sport clothes.

As the leaders assembled for prayer backstage, the president took one look at me and said, "My, Mickie, don't we look sporty?"

Privately I wondered why the Lord hadn't checked me on wearing the outfit. Later I found out that He had permitted me to make a faux pas at the meeting for His own good reasons.

Upon arrival in Encinitas, we checked in to the motel quickly and hurried to Lynne's home. Later that evening, Beverly, Lynne and I were seated in a charming restaurant, enjoying our dinner by candlelight as we shared confidences with each other. One of those little confidences came from Lynne, who laughingly said as she looked at me, "I never expected a minister to come into my home wearing a bright yellow blazer, a royal blue shirt and a white pleated skirt—but here you are!"

Lynne could easily relate to my casual appearance; she herself wore fashionably tight blue jeans. The Lord created a friendship between us before we ever talked about His divine sonship.

Beverly gave Lynne my book *Through a Glass, Darkly* and another to her son and his wife. Later, another daughter who was home from college read the book as well.

The next morning, we headed again to Lynne's home. This time there was a real commotion. Their little dog had disappeared. I prayed with them for its recovery, and God answered our prayer!

After some scouting, the dog was found. Lynne's adorable little grandson was so delighted over the return of his pet.

Next, we had dinner in the family's delightful restaurant. Lynne's son, a gifted chef, prepared the food.

The dishwasher hadn't come to work that evening, so I put on an apron and helped Lynne wash the mountain of dinner dishes. Truthfully, I enjoyed the task. Being with

Lynne and her family was fun! I'm sure it was more fun than seeing the San Diego Zoo!

Besides, I was beginning to understand that God was softening this family's attitude toward me, the minister whom God had sent into their home. I sensed what was coming, but I waited for *God's perfect timing.*

The family members had read my book and learned how God had miraculously healed me of cancer. I was finding acceptance in their hearts. Beverly was enjoying this time with her friends, and so was I. Together we visited La Jolla and the surrounding area.

On our last day together, I asked them all to gather in the living room and form a circle. As they stood with me, I told them of God's great love for them and explained the way to be born again. I told them that God's Son, Jesus Christ, had come to earth in a flesh-and-blood body just like ours. I explained that Jesus had been beaten for our healing and crucified on the Cross for our sins, rising from the grave on the third day.

Then I instructed them to ask the Lord to forgive them of their sins and to invite Him into their hearts. Solemnly, each one in the circle did exactly that. Into their spirits flowed the Holy Spirit of the living Lord Jesus Christ. In that sacred moment, their names were written in the Lamb's Book of Life.

At the same time, I asked the Lord Jesus to heal the beautiful daughter-in-law of cancer. Well, the power of the Lord was present to heal! Her next appointment with the physician provided another X ray, and this time it showed no tumor and no cancer. The Lord had healed the daughter-in-law and saved Lynne and all her household!

Later, Lynne sent me a copy of her daughter's college thesis. It told about a woman from Texas, a minister, and how she affected the entire family.

The thesis almost read as though I were a visitor from another planet! As I read it, my heart overflowed with thanksgiving to God that He had been able to use me in the lives of that precious family.

You know what? God's plans are higher and better than our plans! (Isa. 55:9.) That's why it's so important to be led by Him. He will lead us out of the pitfalls of casualty covenants and straight up into the high places with Him! We need only submit our lives and wills to Him.

10

FINANCIAL COVENANTS

Finances. We all deal with them to one degree or another. God's will is that we prosper financially. However, allowing ourselves to be ruled either by financial worries or the pursuit of financial gain is another matter. We have to be careful that we don't enter into casualty covenants with the enemy in the realm of finances—whether those covenants would make us poor or rich!

Faith—The Currency of Eternity

Money is the currency of our time, but faith is the currency of eternity. To operate in the heavenly realm, we must believe God's Word.

Satan knows this all too well. His first tactic with Eve in the Garden was to alter God's Word. Later, he tried to do the same thing when he tempted Jesus in the wilderness. Today Satan uses the same tactics on us, as he seeks to deceive us into agreeing with his lies. His counsel always contains a compromise of the Word.

To fight the good fight of faith, we need to believe with our hearts—our born-again spirits—and speak God's Word with our mouths over our financial situations. (A good place to start is by speaking the Word with our mouths, *but we also have to believe God's promises in order for them to come to pass.*)

The same Jesus who told His disciples that the Father God would provide for their needs is the same Lord Jesus Christ who tells us today:

> **Seek (aim and strive after) first of all His kingdom, and His righteousness [His way of doing and being right], and then all these things taken together will be given you besides.**
>
> **Matthew 6:33 AMP**

God will not overlook or forget your good deeds; God will reward you well, not only in the life to come, but in *this* life here on earth. Indeed, one of His covenant names is Jehovah Jireh—the Lord will provide.

In Malachi 3:10, God also encourages us to prove Him in the financial area of our lives by tithing and giving. This Scripture helps us understand the spiritual aspect of giving our finances. God's divine promise is that He will abundantly reward those who obey Him in their finances by giving.

HONORING GOD THROUGH GIVING

• • •

Giving into God's work is also a form of worshipping and honoring Him. First Kings 17:8-23 again gives us a great biblical example in the account of Elijah and the widow of Zarephath. God sent Elijah to Zarephath to stay with a widow and her son, who were starving in the midst of a great famine. The widow had planned to use her meager supplies to make one last meal for her and her son before they died.

Elijah admonished her not to fear. And then he had the audacity to ask her to first bake *him* a little loaf of bread before cooking anything for herself and her son! But Elijah also prophesied that if she did so, her flour and oil would not give out until the day the Lord provided rain for the land. The widow chose to honor the word of the Lord by giving her last bit of food to the man of God. In doing so, she opened the way for her miracle.

Basic spiritual principles are operating in this story.

On the widow's part we see these principles at work:

- Resisting the spirit of fear. (Fear negates faith.)
- Giving in order for it to be given unto you. (Luke 6:38.)
- Having faith in God for a miracle of provision.

On Elijah's part we see these principles at work:

- Hearing a *rhema* word from the Lord.
- Being obedient to the Lord.
- Operating in the anointing of God.

As we fulfill the principles of God's Word with a right heart motive, we do not need to beg the Lord for blessings, because He has already prepared them for us.

That was certainly true in the case of the widow of Zarephath. Because of her heart obedience, God supernaturally provided for her and her son in the midst of famine. Then later, He also used Elijah to raise her son from the dead. She was abundantly blessed!

Bobbye Byerly, director of Prayer and Intercession of World Prayer Center and former president of the U.S. Aglow International made this observation: "Poverty is not the state of not having, but the fear of not getting, which causes you to hold on tightly to what you have, rendering you unable to receive. Prosperity is not the state of having, but the understanding that what you need and desire for every area of your life, your heavenly Father will give you. This understanding causes you to hold loosely to what you have, enabling you to receive more in abundance. Remember, God is not moved by need. He is moved by faith." (Ps. 84:11.)

BREAKING A FINANCIAL CASUALTY COVENANT
• • •

A few years ago, I held one of our mini-retreats for college students at our lake house. These retreats were always a time of fellowship and lively discussion, liberally sprinkled with prayer and Bible study.

During one of these discussions, a senior in college named Jeff explained to the group that he had been poor all his life. His parents had divorced, causing a strain on their financial situation. From then on his family always had to conserve their money.

As Jeff grew up in this kind of atmosphere, he unconsciously made a covenant with the enemy to be poor the rest of his life. You see, that's all he knew, so the devil convinced him that poverty would be all he'd ever know. Consequently, Jeff accepted the fact that he was poor—

and he expected always to be. That casualty covenant dogged his steps as he left home to attend college, because in order to go to the reputable Christian college he desired, Jeff had to go into debt, taking out several loans just to pay for tuition and expenses.

During his college years, Jeff began to work with a Christian campus ministry. Then later, he started working for a homeless ministry and an inner-city, low-income ministry.

As time passed, anger built up inside Jeff against Christians who weren't out ministering to the poor. As he became more and more entrenched in his poverty mind-set, he started criticizing his church for focusing on the construction of bigger buildings instead of working with the poor and homeless as Jesus did. As a result, Jeff's heart became prejudiced toward wealthy people, especially wealthy Christians. (You can see the progression of the devil's strategy as he took Jeff down his twilight trail.)

Ironically, Jeff was a finance major with the spiritual gift of giving. After he told me this story, I asked him two questions: "Jeff, if God needed someone to manage money, would He give the position to someone who couldn't handle money? And if God created a person with a giving heart, would He give it to someone who didn't have the means to give?"

I gave Jeff several Scriptures to read and began to explain casualty covenants to him. He meditated on the Scriptures that night and later realized that he had made a covenant to be poor. The next day, in the name of Jesus Christ, Jeff broke his covenant with a spirit of poverty.

Jeff later explained what he had learned about the covenant he had made with the enemy: "I believed the lie that I should be poor and that it's better to give everything away and not prosper financially. I thought God loved me more because I had become poor like the homeless."

The enemy did not like Jeff's new financial freedom, so he attempted to slow him down with illness. But Jeff received prayer and good medical help. He overcame the physical attack and is now employed by a financial firm. He is paying off his school loans and regularly tithing to his church, and the blessings keep coming!

Jeff recently opened a savings account with $1,500. Soon afterwards, he found out that a local missions organization was planning a trip to Venezuela that just happened to cost $1,500.

Jeff felt the Lord calling him to go on this mission trip and take a step of faith by paying for it himself. As Jeff prayed for God's will in this decision, he remembered the Scripture:

"Bring the whole tithe into the storehouse, so that there may be food in My house, and test Me now in this," says the Lord of hosts, "if I will not open for you the windows of heaven, and pour out for you a blessing until there is no more need. Then I will rebuke the devourer for you, so that it may not destroy the fruits of the ground; nor will your vine in the field cast its grapes," says the Lord of hosts.

Malachi 3:10,11 NAS

Jeff realized that the only way he could possibly go to Venezuela was to use the entire amount in his savings account. So that's exactly what he did.

Jeff arranged to take time off from work. He also sent out a letter requesting prayer and fasting support, asking people to invest in his ministry as they were led of the Lord. Everything was set for the mission.

As Jeff prepared to leave, several people gave Jeff money for the trip, even though he never specifically asked for contributions. Then after Jeff returned to the states, his boss gave him a raise.

So in the end, Jeff really came out ahead! He had obeyed God's admonition in Malachi 3:10 to prove His faithfulness. Now he was experiencing God's promise in Ezekiel 34:26 NAS: **And I will cause showers to come down in their season; they will be showers of blessing.**

Jeff learned an important lesson through this experience. He later told me, "Many churches curse you when you don't tithe. But, really, *the purpose of giving is to bless God and to receive God's blessings.*"

Now Jeff understands the truth that God wants to bless us. If we are willing and obedient ambassadors for Christ, we are entitled to all the benefits He has provided for us in His name. Since that is true, would God not see to it that we are abundantly blessed on earth—if we will just lay hold of His benefits by faith?

Then we can say with the Psalmist:

Bless the Lord, O my soul, and *forget none of His benefits;* who pardons all your iniquities; who heals all your diseases; who

redeems your life from the pit; who crowns you with lovingkindness and compassion; who satisfies your years with good things, so that your youth is renewed like the eagle.

Psalm 103:2-5 NAS

A STORY OF NEEDLESS LOSS
• • •

The following is a tragic, true story of a man named Joe. It is a classic example of how a casualty covenant can put a consenting, agreeable person in bondage. Just as dark forces hold humans in bondage to their demonic activity through deception, so, too, was Joe literally imprisoned unjustly as a result of a casualty covenant he made with his shrewd, dishonest employer.

This employer was a wealthy man who was guilty of fraud in his business. He hired Joe to work for him, even though he recognized that Joe was a middle-aged, slow-witted man.

Now, Joe wasn't a bad guy—just one who had suffered financial lack in this world. The wealthy man recognized that he could use this simple man for his own purposes. Meanwhile, poor, bumbling Joe was just grateful to have a job.

Joe had a devout Catholic mother, who was always concerned about her son. She and her priest prayed continually for him. It seemed a blessing to both the mother and the priest that Joe had found steady employment.

Unfortunately, Joe's employer had other plans. He was facing certain imprisonment for his fraudulent activities. Then it occurred to him that if he could persuade someone else to admit to the crime instead of him, he could escape his punishment.

With this in mind, the wealthy man began to spend time cultivating Joe's confidence. After a while, in a very private conversation, Joe's employer presented this proposal: "If you will say that you committed my crime and go to prison in my place for approximately two years, I will take care of you for the rest of your life. You will never have need of anything."

Joe contemplated this proposition. He wanted to please his employer, who had been good to him. Joe thought about the prospect of spending two years in prison compared to enjoying financial prosperity for the rest of his life. He considered the employment problems he had always experienced.

This appeared to Joe to be a way out of his financial troubles. In reality, it was a snare, causing Joe to make a deal with the devil.

The wealthy man and Joe agreed that Joe would take the rap and go to prison. At that moment, Joe made a covenant with a lie. By biblical definition, Joe had truly become a simple man: **A prudent man foreseeth the evil, and hideth himself: but the simple pass on, and are punished** (Prov. 22:3).

Joe's mother and her priest prayed fervently for Joe's deliverance from prison. They didn't know that by a choice of his own will, Joe had agreed to spend time in prison for a crime he had not committed.

How often does a holy God get blamed for a person's mistakes?

This true story does not get better. While Joe was in prison serving his employer's time, the wealthy man died. Of course, there was no record of his promising Joe anything.

When Joe emerged from prison after two years, he was a poorer man with a prison record, which further handicapped him from gainful employment.

The mother and the priest's prayers had apparently gone unanswered. We can guess that this failure to receive what they had asked God for fractured their faith. Joe wasn't the only casualty of the covenant he had made with a lie.

(You see, until children reach the age of account-ability, parents can usually intercede for them success-fully. But it is often deeply painful for parents to realize that their older children can, by a choice of their own will, short-circuit God's answer to the parents' prayers for them. That's exactly what happened with Joe's mother.)

You may be facing financial difficulties in your life. But you will never find your way out of poverty and lack by making covenants with the enemy, as Joe did. The path to financial prosperity lies only in agreeing with what *God* has to say in His Word about finances.

THE BLUE CONVERTIBLE

• • •

We can see this same principle of agreeing with God's Word instead of Satan's lies in the case of a lovely young woman whom I met several years ago. The story of how God blessed her is a manifestation of two divine promises:

192

Delight thyself also in the Lord; and he shall give thee the desires of thine heart.

Psalm 37:4

Again I say unto you, That if two of you shall agree on earth as touching any thing that they shall ask, it shall be done for them of my Father which is in heaven.

Matthew 18:19

A dear friend brought this young woman to my home. She was young, petite and pretty, with beautiful, dark hair and eyes. She was willing to freely give her time and Spanish language skills to help translate my book *Through a Glass, Darkly.*

As we worked together, the young woman told me about her needs. She was a schoolteacher with a malfunctioning car—a Fiat Spider convertible. But she was also a woman who truly believed in Almighty God. Hebrews 11:1 was a reality in her life: **Now faith is the substance of things hoped for, the evidence of things not seen.**

The young woman confessed that she desired another car, so we discussed God's promise in Psalm 37:4: **He shall give thee the desires of thine heart.** I suggested that we pray in agreement for a specific car for her. She thought I was a little "off the wall" but decided to pray with me because she really desired a better car and knew that prayer would work.

We prayed specifically for a Fiat Spider convertible. At this time, she was riding her bike to work. She was waiting on God's timing for her car, and as we all know, waiting is never easy.

One morning, the young lady was riding her bicycle on the way to work when suddenly she turned her head and saw an almost-new, blue Fiat Spider convertible parked in front of a house! She made a U-turn, parked her bike, knocked on the door and asked the woman who opened it, "Is that car for sale?"

Surprised, the woman replied, "How did you know? I just hung up the phone after talking to my husband, and he told me to put a 'For Sale' sign on it and call the newspapers to advertise."

My friend explained to the woman that God had caused her to inquire. My friend inspected the car and discovered that it was in excellent condition. It was a new model with low mileage. (Her old Fiat convertible was an older model with many more miles on it.) The owners of the car sold it to her under blue-book value because the metallic top had faded.

This young schoolteacher waited for God's answer, believing He had heard our prayer of agreement. She also "put her feet to her faith" by cooperating with the Holy Spirit when He nudged her to walk up to a stranger's house and ask the owner about the Fiat Spider convertible parked outside.

My friend didn't let the devil rob her with doubt and unbelief. She made no covenant with him. She stayed in agreement with God's Word, which says, **Every good and perfect gift is from above, coming down from the Father of the heavenly lights, who does not change like shifting shadows** (James 1:17 NIV).

This car was a real testimony to all the young woman's Christian friends about the importance of waiting on

God. Waiting is not always easy to do, but it is a must in many situations. My friend persevered and received the desire of her heart.

So while waiting on God to answer your prayers, be careful not to unconsciously make an agreement with an evil spirit to settle for anything less than *God's* answer. If you do, you could be cheated out of God's blessings!

A Temple That Is Holy—*Not* "Holey"!

The devil usually tries to convince us that we shouldn't drive nice cars or wear attractive clothing; he seeks to convince us that "holey" garments speak of "holy" hearts. When we buy into these subtle lies of the enemy, we disappoint our Father's giving heart.

For example, the temple that God required Solomon to build contained a foundation of costly stones, and the entire house was overlaid with gold. (1 Kings 6,7.) It was *not* a shabby place!

Well, when we invite Jesus Christ into our hearts, our bodies become the temple of God. (2 Cor. 6:16.) Personal experience has taught me that God doesn't require us to look shabby either. Sometimes we may even need to polish our "temples." As one minister said, "Even a barn looks better when it is painted."

In the final analysis, however, **The Lord seeth not as man seeth; for man looketh on the outward appearance, but the Lord looketh on the heart** (1 Sam. 16:7). Therefore, our most important endeavor should be to keep our hearts clean of any agreements with that old serpent, the devil, who is totally corrupt.

Instead, we must trust in the integrity of God's promise to bless us financially. As we honor Him through our tithing and giving, He will provide for us abundantly and make our temples shine inside *and* out to His glory!

1·1

DISCERNING
SPIRITUAL GUIDANCE

God has many supernatural ways to help guide us
through life. He gives us the inner guidance, comfort and
revelation of the Holy Spirit. He sometimes warns us
through dreams or visions or speaks to us through the
gift of prophecy. At times He even sends angels with a
message from heaven.

GOD'S PLAN FOR JOSEPH

God guides us in supernatural ways because He has
a plan and purpose for each of us. Let's look more
closely at how this works, for example, in the life of
Joseph. (Gen. 37:6-10.)

Now, God had a divine plan for Joseph's life. But he
was sold as a slave by his own brothers. He was also
unjustly thrown into an Egyptian prison many miles from
home. But God's plan still prevailed, as Joseph explained
years later to his brothers—after they had come to him
looking for help:

Now therefore be not grieved, nor angry with yourselves, that ye sold me hither: for God did send me before you to preserve life. For these two years hath the famine been in the land: and yet there are five years, in the which there shall neither be earing nor harvest.

And God sent me before you to preserve you a posterity in the earth, and to save your lives by a great deliverance.

Genesis 45:5-7

Through God's divine hand of guidance, Joseph rose to a position of power second only to Pharaoh, and he was able to save the lives of thousands during seven years of severe famine.

DREAMS AND VISIONS
* * *

Joseph is an example of one whom God guided at times through prophetic dreams. Acts 2:17 says that in the last days, many of God's people will receive this kind of supernatural guidance:

And it shall come to pass in the last days, saith God, I will pour out of my Spirit upon all flesh: and your sons and your daughters shall prophesy, and your young men shall see visions, and your old men shall dream dreams.

But God is not the only one who seeks to guide through dreams. The prince of the power of the air, Satan, desires to craft our dreams for us. His purpose is to direct our destiny. If we accept his lying dreams and expect them to become a reality, he will try to cause occurrences in our lives to conform to these planned catastrophes.

The dreams Satan plants in our minds hide his desire to dominate and control our lives. In other words, we may think these dreams are our thoughts since we indeed dreamed them. These satanic dreams are as dangerous and deceptive as is putting our trust in fortunetelling and horoscopes.

If we believe the future this type of soothsayer predicts, we open the door to the evil one because we are seeking knowledge from his evil empire. This is an abomination to the Lord. And our disobedience gives Satan permission to afflict us, which can result in our making casualty covenants.

As you can see, dreams are not always reliable. Unless God's Word and the principles of His kingdom agree with a dream, it is best to trash it! Make no agreement with ungodly dreams; put them totally out of your thoughts, giving no place to the devil.

Many have lost their lives, loved ones and cherished hopes through the demonic maneuver of false dreams. On the other hand, God-given dreams are direct and usually repeated. Although they may bring a warning, they also give a sense of His true peace. But when Satan is the source of the dream, there is either fear and anxiety or sometimes a false sense of peace.

A third type of dream incorporates daily activities from our everyday thoughts and tired bodies. Such dreams are neither from God nor from Satan and usually do not carry much spiritual significance. Ecclesiastes 5:7

AMP warns us, **In the multitude of dreams there is futility and worthlessness.**

The remedy for deception in any area, including dreams, is to speak aloud the promises of our Creator with faith in our hearts for ourselves and for others. His holy Word is a hammer that will break into pieces all the lies of the evil one. (Jer. 23:29.)

Visions, in contrast to dreams, are divine manifestations in which a person sees into the realm of the spirit. God gives them as He chooses, and they always agree with His holy Word. We must also judge visions by God's written Word because, just as with dreams, it is possible for the arch-deceiver to deceive Christians with visions as one of his dirty tricks from his infamous stockpile.

Just because you encounter the supernatural, you cannot assume its source is the heavenly realm. Remember, two powers operate in the supernatural: the kingdom of heaven and Satan's evil empire.

Visions from the Lord are priceless treasures given to bless, instruct and guide us. (Acts 27:23.) However, we must be vigilant to discern the origin of a vision. Remember,

> **Be sober, be vigilant; because your adversary the devil, as a roaring lion, walketh about, seeking whom he may devour.**
>
> **1 Peter 5:8**

THINGS THAT GO BUMP IN THE NIGHT
• • •

I know from personal experience about Satan's deceptive dreams. When I was dying of terminal cancer, I had two small sons to raise; so naturally, I wanted to live.

However, after undergoing three surgeries with discouraging results, I began to lose some of my will to fight.

One night I dreamed of my death. In the dream, my body was laid out in a coffin. Strangely, a great, almost tangible peace permeated the entire scene. Death meant no more suffering, no more pain, no more struggling—just permanent peace.

Awakening the next morning, I easily discerned the source of the dream: Satan was using the bait of his false peace to persuade me to accept a spirit of death. If I had made this casualty covenant with him, I could have died prematurely years ago and missed the joy of raising my sons and serving the Lord in this lifetime.

In our weakest moments, the devil offers his solutions, but they always lead to disaster!

You may ask me, "How did you discern between the false peace in the dream and the true gift of peace from the Prince of Peace?"

Well, according to 1 Corinthians 12:10, the Holy Spirit gives us the ability to discern spirits. By the operation of this gift, we can know by the Spirit of God what kind of spirit is involved in a particular situation.[1] This is the gift I received from the Holy Spirit concerning my dream.

FALSE VISIONS
. . .

As I've said, Satan tries to deceive people through lying dreams and also through false visions. I saw an example of how this happens recently when I spoke at a women's luncheon in Houston. As I concluded my talk on casualty covenants, I noticed a young woman who was crying. Seeing her distress, I walked over to her. As I ministered to the woman, I realized she had mistakenly made a casualty covenant because of a counterfeit vision—a vision straight from the pit of hell.

The following is the woman's account of her vision and the gripping fear that followed it:

> I had a vision over fifteen years ago of going to heaven and talking to Jesus. I heard the heavenly angelic songs. I experienced peace that I had never felt before. But as I was talking to Jesus, He told me that I would contract hepatitis and that it would bring me into His presence.
>
> Now, I am a nurse. So every time I worked with a patient or knew someone with hepatitis, I thought: *Is this when or how I'll get it?* My husband recently had some test results that suggested hepatitis. I thought that maybe he had the disease and that I would get it from him.
>
> Not long ago, I also had eye surgery resulting in the complication of double vision. I was recently talking to my mother on the phone about it and told her that I had always imagined myself losing my eyesight and had feared I would go blind.

A supernatural vision had dramatically deceived this young woman into receiving spirits of infirmity. The Bible tells us,

> **Satan does it all the time, dressing up as a beautiful angel of light. So it shouldn't surprise us when his servants masquerade as servants of God.**
>
> **But they're not getting by with anything. They'll pay for it in the end.**
>
> **2 Corinthians 11:14,15** THE MESSAGE

The woman was a precious child of God who wanted to please Him. But her lack of knowledge of God's Word—that He wants His children in good health—made her vulnerable, and she agreed with the devil's counterfeit vision. Fortunately, that day she broke both casualty covenants related to her physical well-being in the name of Jesus!

Reality is based on what God's Word says, not on our experiences, no matter how real they seem to be. The apostle Peter received many visions. He was with Jesus on the Mount of Transfiguration when Jesus' clothing suddenly became as white as snow. (Mark 9:3-7.) Peter watched a cloud overshadow them. He heard a voice come out of the cloud, saying, **This is my beloved Son: hear him** (v. 7).

Peter, who had seen and heard God and who had been with Jesus, later wrote: **We have also a more sure word of prophecy; whereunto ye do well that ye take heed, as unto a light that shineth in a dark place** (2 Peter 1:19). Peter was saying that the Word is a more real and sure revelation and light unto our lives. The Word of God is more reliable than our experiences, dreams or visions.

MARTYRDOM OR PREMATURE DEATH?

Martyrdom raises a similar issue: some Christians may be called to be martyred, but others have been deceived by evil, counterfeit spirits.

Instead of thinking about how you're going to die for God's glory, concentrate on *living* for His glory! For some people, death can provide a premature way out of the difficulties of this life. But Jesus said, **Occupy till I come** (Luke 19:13). To occupy means "to dwell in, hold or engage one's self in."[2]

Beware of becoming a martyr—of sacrificing your life unnecessarily. God has already given us a Savior, His Son, so you don't qualify as a savior!

We know there are true martyrs, who lose their lives for the sake of the gospel, and our hearts are ever grateful to them. The book of Revelation speaks of the blood of the martyrs of Jesus. (Rev. 17:6.) However, there are also those Satan deceives into suffering unnecessarily and even dying prematurely through evil spirits of martyrdom.

How many noble people have bought into this satanic lie throughout the years? But we shouldn't die early—let us *live* for God's honor and glory!

VOICES AND DIVINE VISITATIONS

After hearing or reading stories of how the Lord or angels appeared to other Christians, sometimes sincere believers are tempted to get into a crisis in the hope of having a divine visitation. This can lead to the sin of presumption, and God cannot honor sin.

For instance, a young woman heard stories of how God spoke to different people in her church. She desperately wanted to hear from God herself. This became an obsession with her.

One evening, as the young woman sat in her usual place at church, she suddenly heard words spoken to her. It was as though a person stood beside her, speaking in an audible voice. The words pertained to another desire within her heart—the desire to be married. The voice said, *The young man walking down the aisle will be your husband.*

In her excitement over hearing the supernatural promise, she could barely keep herself from embracing the young, disheveled man who was walking toward the altar.

As she stared at him, he looked back at her. Their eyes met, and the romance began.

What the woman didn't know was that the young man had an extremely checkered background: drugs, promiscuous sex—the whole nine yards! But despite the warning signs, the young woman thought, *Hey, God will make it all okay!* She agreed with the words she believed God had spoken to her—that this man was to be her husband.

So the wedding came and went. Shortly after their marriage, more problems surfaced. Not only did the husband continue his drug abuse, but at times, he became violent toward his bride. Her parents became concerned about the deteriorating appearance and the well-being of their beautiful daughter.

Much prayer was sown. In the meantime, even more hidden things came to light about the groom.

This was *not* a marriage made in heaven! The young woman had eagerly desired to hear from God, and Satan had taken advantage of her naiveté and given her a word "from God."

Divorce was inevitable. Husbands are not to be violent toward their wives, verbally or physically, nor are they to indulge in illicit drug use. (Mal. 2:16.) This young

Christian wife was devastated. Her husband had chosen drugs instead of her. She was heartbroken. She didn't know that she had made a covenant with a lying spirit because of her strong desire to hear from God and have a husband. Now her dreams lay like ashes around her feet, and she wondered if she could ever trust God again.

Then the young woman read my book *Through a Glass, Darkly.* Slowly she began to receive understanding that she had been deceived into making a casualty covenant. With this revelation knowledge, she repented of her presumption as she received God's love to heal her wounded heart. Hope and trust in her Father God bloomed once more, and she was able to love again.

PREVAILING PRAYER AND A RESCUE ON THE FREEWAY
* * *

Frankly, I'm not seeking to hear from angels, because Satan himself is transformed into an angel of light (2 Cor. 11:14). However, at our Father God's appointing, angels can speak. We just have to be careful with whom we agree.

For example, when Peter was arrested, bound in chains and thrust in prison, the church prayed fervently for him. And an angel delivered Peter from prison in answer to those prayers.

Here's what happened. Peter was sleeping between two soldiers, when suddenly an angel of the Lord appeared beside him and awakened him.

And, behold, the angel of the Lord came upon him, and a light shined in the prison: and he smote Peter on the side, and raised

**him up, saying, Arise up quickly. And his
chains fell off from his hands.**

Acts 12:7

So we can see from Scripture that angels do occasionally speak. I actually experienced this one cold, wet New
Year's Eve. I heard my angel speak a divine warning to
me, but I was unable to discern who was speaking.

It all started that night, when the telephone rang in
my home. I answered it quickly to keep from disturbing
my husband, who was sleeping on the sofa. I was
surprised to hear the voice of a young friend of mine.

She said, "April and I are going to midnight Communion services. Will you go with us?"

It was about 11 P.M., and I wondered if we still had
time to make it there. My friend assured me that they
would come immediately and we would drive straight to
the service. I agreed and rushed to change clothes.

In the midst of preparation, a question from an
unseen source at my right side asked, "Have you prayed
over this?" Turning this unexpected question over in my
mind, I decided the question must be from the evil
empire, for surely it would not be necessary to pray about
attending church Communion services.

Hearing the sound of the car horn, I did not have
time to ponder the source of this intrusion into my
thoughts any longer. It was time to leave. Joining the
young women in the car, I experienced some misgivings
when April, our driver, backed her car out of our driveway
and into a tree.

We checked the tree and the car. Finding nothing
damaged, we piled back into the front seat and snuggled

close together because the car heater was malfunctioning. The windshield wipers didn't work very well either. This made our visibility rather poor, leaving us no choice but to keep the windows rolled down.

As we proceeded onto the freeway, the three of us had a difference of opinion about which route to church was fastest. Finally, April left the freeway and began traveling swiftly on the feeder street.

Suddenly, April made an unexpected fast turn onto an elevated one-way express lane. As we arrived at the top of this express lane, we immediately realized we were in a one-way lane going the wrong way!

We stopped dead still, unable to turn around or go forward because of oncoming cars. Their lights blinded us. One could almost see the headlines: "Three women traveling the wrong way instantly killed in a head-on collision on New Year's Eve."

I had one thought: *Pray!* I told the girls to join hands with me, and we bowed our heads together. I prayed, "Lord, send immediate help in Jesus Christ's name. We are in big trouble here. Thank You, Lord. Amen."

As we lifted our heads, we were surprised to see no lights from oncoming cars. However, directly in front of us was a parked car with police lights. A uniformed man walked over to April's window. He was very calm, almost casual, as he asked, "Do you need help?"

In our relief, we all talked at once, saying, *"Yes, yes, yes!"*

The man said, "I'll keep my car parked in front of yours. That will block the cars from coming up to the top of this express lane while you turn your car around and descend."

Speedily, April turned around, descended the elevated ramp, parked on the side of the road and waited for the policeman's car. We expected a ticket or a warning from our helper. But it never came. He never passed us. We never saw him again. Was he an angel in human form? We never knew.

All three of us know that our Father God sent help in answer to our prayer. Evidently, Satan had a plan to destroy us, but God had a plan to rescue us.

When I neglected to pray earlier concerning traveling with my young friends on New Year's Eve, I missed the warning that had been sent—not by an evil spirit, but I believe by my guardian angel. Scripture reveals that all believers have God-appointed angels to minister for them.

Are they not all ministering spirits, sent forth to minister for them who shall be heirs of salvation?

Hebrews 1:14

It is up to us to grow in the knowledge of God's Word and His ways so we can accurately discern His leading. That's how we keep ourselves from being deceived by Satan's counterfeit manifestations, which are designed to lead us into covenants that will rob us of God's best. Remember, the devil seeks to dominate us, but God seeks to guide us to our destiny in Him!

12

SPIRITUAL WARFARE

God wants us to live free from every bondage and casualty covenant that the enemy would use to ensnare us. Therefore, He gives us divine weapons of warfare by which we can enforce the victory Jesus bought for us on the Cross. (2 Cor. 10:4,5.)

God also provides us with divine guidelines in His Word to help us thwart the strategies of the enemy. For instance, we have the authority and the responsibility to break the power of all evil words and curses spoken against us. We must also be alert not to undermine or corrupt the souls of others with our own negative words.

As you learn how to conduct spiritual warfare, you may even want to become a part of a prayer team in order to break curses.

OUR AUTHORITY IN JESUS' NAME
* * *

God has given us the authority to break the power of evil words and curses! Jesus said to His disciples: **Behold! I have given you authority and power...**

over *all* the power that the enemy [possesses] and nothing shall in any way harm you (Luke 10:19 AMP).

Demons are subject to believers today just as demons were subject to the disciples then, but many Christians seem unaware that they possess this spiritual authority over the enemy.

Always remember this: *Christians proceed in life from a basis of victory—not defeat.* The Lord Jesus Christ obtained our victory for us.

> **And having disarmed the powers and authorities [Satan's entire evil kingdom], he made a public spectacle of them, triumphing over them by the cross.**
>
> **Colossians 2:15 NIV**

Because we haven't earned this spiritual victory, many times we are slow to accept that we have it. It is difficult to give up our natural reasoning, which says, *If I could just become more special to God, I might be worthy to use His authority.*

The devil doesn't want us to know the truth—that God has already given His righteousness and His authority to each of His followers through Jesus, the divine Son of God:

> **God made him who had no sin to be sin for us, who had no sin, so that in him we might become the righteousness of God.**
>
> **2 Corinthians 5:21 NIV**

Jesus provided us with the use of His name in order to command demons to leave, be bound, confused, forbidden to speak and so forth. Jesus' name represents

His character, His righteousness, His sacrifice on the Cross at Calvary for all humans and His resurrection from the dead.

And as we have already discussed, we can use the power in the name of Jesus to break personal casualty covenants we may have made with any of Satan's lies.

As believers, we must accept the truth about our responsibility to exercise our authority over the enemy. Jesus said, **These attesting signs will accompany those who believe: in My name they will drive out demons** (Mark 16:17 AMP). *Notice, Christians do not have authority over another person's will.* Are you a believer? Then you are to drive out *demons* in Jesus' name!

MY PERSONAL SPIRITUAL WARFARE
. . .

Scripture tells us that we are not to worry about tomorrow, because there is enough evil for today. (Matt. 6:34.) Therefore, I seek to remember each day to bind Satan's influence and his demons from myself, my husband, our relatives and all their relatives, as well as all matters pertaining to any of us.

With the words of my mouth, I forbid Satan in the name of Jesus Christ to vent his wrath, vengeance or retaliation through his emissaries against us, our habitations, our relationships and our finances. Also, I cast down and bind all psychic prayers, all forms of witchcraft and all forms of curses that would come against us, our properties and our possessions.

Finally, I resist anxiety and worry by consciously casting my cares upon the Lord. (1 Peter 5:7.) And I do all this *every single day.* It is my personal spiritual warfare.

CORPORATE SPIRITUAL WARFARE
. . .

Next, I'm ready to conduct spiritual warfare on behalf of others. Participating in corporate warfare can produce wonderful answers to prayer, such as in the following example.

Because I am a personal prayer intercessor for the Peter Wagner family and the World Prayer Center, I often receive impressions concerning them while in prayer. During one particular prayer time, I was impressed by the Holy Spirit with the word *curse.* Thinking there might be curses against the Prayer Center or against the Wagners, I passed this information on to them.

Later, I received a letter from the Wagners that read, in part:

> An amazing event happened at the World Prayer Center during the International Conference on Prayer and Spiritual Warfare. This was totally orchestrated by God in answer to your prayers, even though you probably knew nothing specifically as you were praying. On the Thursday morning of the Conference, April 23, Bobbye Byerly was leading the intercessors, and she felt moved to take them out to pray on the site at the World Prayer Center.

Here the story is continued by Jean Steffenson, President of the Native American Resource Center:

> They had a fantastic time, but when they finished, Bobbye told me what had happened, and I said it would have been better if they had included Native American intercessors with them. Fortunately, there were in attendance

some dozen Native Americans. Some of the Native American leaders and I came into the intercession room. As we prayed, God revealed to one of them that a medicine man sometime in the unknown past had buried a fetish of some kind on that very land and cursed the white man who would occupy it. Jay Swallow and the other Native Americans volunteered to go to the land and take the initiative to break the curse, which he and a group did. They would not allow any whites to participate, but when they finished, a native leader took a handful of dirt and poured it into Bobbye's hand as a token "deed of trust" from the Indians to the whites for the World Prayer Center property.

Peter Wagner continued in his letter:

> When many of us heard this, we knew for sure that it had been the most important element of the whole World Prayer Center project, bar none. This was totally orchestrated by God. Without it, whatever we did in the World Prayer Center would be operating on three cylinders at the best. Satan wanted to keep the curse secret, and he probably would have succeeded were it not for your faithful and fervent prayers.

Why is corporate prayer so powerful? Because it focuses the corporate authority of a group of believers against one target: the thief who comes to kill, steal and destroy. We have authority over him!

I have given you authority to trample on snakes and scorpions and to overcome all the power of the enemy; nothing will harm you.

Luke 10:19 NIV

CURSED OBJECTS

Not only do we need to cleanse our hearts and bodies so we can present ourselves as a living sacrifice before

God (Rom. 12:1), but we also need to spiritually "cleanse" our homes and the objects in them by the name and the blood of Jesus. Our bodies and our homes are our territories, and the devil wants to snatch away anything that belongs to us.

If a person opens the door to the enemy through sin, spiritual slothfulness and so forth, the devil will try to stick his foot in it. One way he does that is by having one of his witches, warlocks, fortunetellers or anyone else involved in the occult put a curse on that person. But a more subtle tactic he uses is to put a demonic curse on an object and whoever owns that object.

C. Peter Wagner says in his book *Warfare Prayer,* "Real demons do attach themselves to animals, idols, brass rings, trees, mountains, and buildings as well as to any number and variety of manufactured and natural objects."[1]

Carol, a Christian friend and neighbor, was a director for a private tutoring service in Texas for many years. She regularly dealt with problem students and often noticed a connection between these kids and the occult.

One time as she was tutoring a teenage boy, she realized he had a hard time concentrating. Carol also observed that he was not receptive to the gospel in the slightest. Then she noticed an astrological sign on a gold bracelet that the boy was wearing on his arm. As Carol inquired about this unusual piece of jewelry, she found out someone had given the bracelet to the boy as a gift.

The boy explained to Carol that a complete stranger had come up to him in a laundromat one day and given him the bracelet. When the boy had first seen the stranger, a woman, her back was toward him. Because of her long, flowing hair, he had thought the woman must be young and beautiful. But when she turned around to face him, the boy had been stunned to realize she was much older than he'd first thought. The elderly woman had come up to the boy and offered him the bracelet, assuring him that it would bring him good luck.

After hearing this story, Carol asked her student to take the bracelet off, but he absolutely refused. He confessed that he would surely die if he ever took it off. The boy admitted that the old woman had never told him that he would die but that he had felt this once he put on the bracelet.

You see, many people don't realize that the devil whispers to them in the first person. He knows that people are naturally more ready to accept their own opinions than the thoughts of someone else. If people think that an idea is their own, why wouldn't they believe it?

Understanding that the boy really believed this lie of premature death, Carol prayed privately that the bracelet would break and fall off his arm.

One day the student showed up without the bracelet. Carol asked him what happened to it. The boy said it had fallen off in his sleep, and he had never put it on again. Once the bracelet was removed, the boy's difficulty concentrating and his blindness to the gospel vanished. He soon invited the Lord into his heart.

Carol believes that the old woman who gave that boy the bracelet may have been a witch and had most likely put a curse on it.

The Bible confirms the fact that physical objects can be cursed:

Did not Achan son of Zerah commit a trespass in the matter of taking accursed things [devoted to destruction] and wrath fall on all the congregation of Israel? And he did not perish alone in his perversity and iniquity.

Joshua 22:20 AMP

I suggest that you ask the Lord to reveal to you if there is a curse on anything you own, whether you purchased it in the United States or in some other country. Make sure your home is cleansed of anything that would leave an open door through which the enemy could try to bind or harass you.

PSYCHIC PRAYERS

• • •

Many Christians understand that in the occult realm, witches and warlocks can convey psychic prayers through chants and curses. Unfortunately, most Christians do *not* understand that they themselves can unknowingly do the same thing. Those who get outside the boundaries of God's Word can unknowingly pray in league with evil spirits.

In other words, rather than praying God's Word over someone, people might pray according to their own carnal desires and ideas—that, for example, God would punish the person or so forth.

Most psychic prayers bring oppression from the evil realm to the person being prayed for. The person may feel like he's under an umbrella of negative thoughts.

When we seek to control and manipulate people through our prayers, we are on the evil empire's dangerous ground. This is one reason it is so important that we make sure our prayers line up with God's Word.

God created humans with a free will to choose. Of course, His way is freedom, whereas Satan's way produces nothing but bondage. The devil uses lies and deceptions to capture humans for his evil purposes. That's how he tricks people—even Christians—to choose his way.

Therefore, we as Christians must be careful to pray for people in alignment with God's will and His Word.

Now, the correct way to pray is to address our Father God in heaven in the name of Jesus Christ; we don't just send prayers out into the atmosphere. We must pray with pure heart motives. We are not permitted to control other human spirits.

I teach a monthly Bible study in Texas. Occasionally, a person with a controlling spirit will attend our meetings. One such woman came faithfully to the meetings. At first, she was helpful. But as time went on, she made increasingly strong suggestions concerning my ministry. Because I did not yield to the controlling spirit, she became frustrated and began to attack me personally.

One of her attacks concerned a decision I had made after much prayer earlier to accept love offerings from Bible study members. These offerings would help finance some of my missionary travels. I knew this decision was scriptural, for the Bible says that the laborer is worthy of his hire. (Luke 10:7; 1 Tim. 5:18.)

The woman did not believe I should receive love offerings from Bible study members. She called other members of the study group, convincing them I was in error. She would call them on the phone to agree with her in prayer that God would put a stop to it. Meanwhile, I was unaware of this woman's anger; however, I did sense spiritual oppression and experience a vague, physical feeling of sickness I could not explain.

As I prayed for understanding, I intuitively recognized the Holy Spirit's voice, directing me to pick up a book I had read many years before—*The Latent Power of the Soul* by Watchman Nee. Nee explains the danger of directing our prayers toward the person for whom we are praying instead of to the heavenly Father:

> Instead of directing your prayer towards God, you concentrate on your thought, your expectation, and your wish and send them out to your friend as a force....
>
> Even though you do not know hypnosis, what you have secretly done has fulfilled the law of hypnotism. You have released your psychic force to perform this act.
>
> ...In appearance you are praying, but in actuality you are oppressing that person with your psychic power.[2]

God answered my prayer for knowledge about the source of my sickness by directing me to read what Watchman Nee had to say about the Christian and the psychic force. Nee says that he personally has experienced ill effects stemming from prayers directed toward him by other people.

After I understood this, I began to resist those psychic prayers, asking God to free me from their effects. In doing so, I was healed. Needless to say, it hurt to see my friends drawn into this web of deceit against me. But in God's grace, I was able to forgive them. And later God brought about reconciliation.

There is no doubt that people need help and counsel. But God has provided the help they need in the Bible and by His Holy Spirit. The source of our true help is from Almighty God, not from the counterfeit realm of "helpful" prayers.

Anything done by psychic force from soulish power will not permanently strengthen the recipient of such prayers. Although the person may say he is helped, it is of a transient nature. On the other hand, the power of true prayer causes lasting profit in a person's life.

So beware of the tricks of the evil empire seeking to ensnare you and yours through the subtle use of psychic prayers. **Remember, where the Spirit of the Lord is, there is liberty** (2 Cor. 3:17).

THE TONGUE TRAP

You may think there is no harm in words. But the truth is, saying wrong words with your mouth and believing those words in your heart can prove to be very detrimental to your life! Let me give you an illustration of how it happens. My friend Quin Sherrer described this story to me:

> My friend JoAnne was driving me to my speaking engagement in Lexington, Kentucky. We had called for directions on how to get to the big, old colonial home where we were to stay. The woman who gave us directions knew how to get there but didn't know street names. Therefore, her directions were rather complex: "Turn at the blue house; go two blocks to the horse farm; turn right"—you get the picture.

We drove slowly, looking for every place we were to turn. Trying to find our way without street names and only landmarks to guide us was very confusing.

After a while we came to a stop sign. To the right of the intersection was a caution sign. We stopped and looked. Neither of us saw any cars coming down the steep hill. JoAnne put her foot on the accelerator to proceed across the country road. Suddenly, we sideswiped a small compact car that we didn't see until the last moment.

The driver of the compact car was a young woman. She jumped out of her car to come see if we were all right just as we jumped out to check on her.

"I have always said I would have a wreck at this corner," the young woman told us. "There have been so many car wrecks here. It is a very dangerous intersection. I've said over and over that one day I'd be in a collision here myself."

"Well, you got what you said!" JoAnne told her.

After we determined both cars were still drivable and no one was hurt, we exchanged addresses and the names of our insurance companies. As we talked, JoAnne and I looked in the backseat of her car and noticed two car seats. The young woman informed us that she was the mother of twins. How glad we were that those twin babies weren't riding in the backseat, for that was exactly where our car had hit hers!

We were certainly glad that no one had been seriously hurt in the collision, although both cars sustained damage. But the fact remains that this woman, who had said and believed she would someday have a wreck at this particular intersection, actually got what she said!

Oftentimes people blame God for their misfortunes. But the truth is, the crisis is often of their own making, brought about through their own words and through wrong choices influenced by the devil.

PARENTAL WORD CURSES

• • •

We can see from Quin's account that people's words can carry curses or blessings. Sometimes this is even true with parents. Parents who love their children can unknowingly put curses on them with their words.

James 3:5 says, **Even so the tongue is a little member, and boasteth great things. Behold, how great a matter a little fire kindleth!**

After speaking on casualty covenants to a group of women at a church in Houston, I had an opportunity to minister to one woman who had been a victim of parental word curses.

This woman's testimony highlights the damage a parent's words can bring to a child.

> Mickie had us pray and ask God to reveal to us what was preventing our healing. In my case, I was suffering from two rheumatic diseases. Due to a deterioration of my immune system from the disease, I also experienced a lot of pain and frequent illnesses. What came to me instantly were words that were spoken repeatedly over me by my mother as I was growing up. She said things like, *"You'll never amount to anything!"*
>
> *"You'll never be able to make it in the world because you're too weak and sickly!"*
>
> *"You're so stupid, you can't see what's in front of your face!"*
>
> *"You have no common sense!"*
>
> *"You're dumb!"*
>
> I have now overcome anorexia and bulimia, but as I was growing up my mother always, always used to say that I was too fat and needed to lose weight. I lost 58 pounds when I was only 4'9" tall. At age ten, I got very sick. My dieting had begun at seven. My top weight at high school

graduation was 115 pounds at 5'4". Later in my adult life, I battled eating disorders for seven years, but God miraculously has delivered me!

This woman's story shows us that when another verbally abuses us, it can cripple our personalities—if we accept the abuser's statements as the truth and make a covenant with the person's destructive words. Romans 3:4 warns us not to do that: **Yea, let God be true, but every man a liar.**

This woman had to use the name of Jesus to break the power of curses spoken over her before she could walk in freedom and good health.

I know of another woman who grew up thinking she was stupid. She struggled with this wounding thought most of her adult life. She explained to me that as a child, her father told her, "Don't ask any questions—people will know how stupid you are!"

Even after the woman was saved, these condemning words reverberated in her memory. But as soon as her heavenly Father opened her eyes to the truth *that she was not stupid*, she forgave her earthly father. With forgiveness came her complete healing.

Both these women had been lied to; both suffered because of those lies. John 8:44 tells us the source of such lies:

> **Ye are of your father the devil, and the lusts of your father ye will do. He was a murderer from the beginning, and abode not in the truth, because there is no truth in him. When he speaketh a lie, he speaketh of his own: for he is a liar, and the father of it.**

When the Father God opened these two women's understanding to the truth, they broke the word curses their parents had ignorantly spoken over them. Unfortunately, their mental images of themselves had been crippled for years before they walked in the light of God's love.

Ask the Holy Spirit to reveal to you if you need to break the power of word curses spoken over you in the past. Just as importantly, ask Him to help you set a guard over your own mouth, for **every idle word that men shall speak, they shall give account thereof in the day of judgment** (Matt. 12:36). Finally, exercise your authority in the name of Jesus over every demonic attack that comes against you. Wage a good warfare as a faithful soldier of Jesus Christ!

13

THE PROMISED SEED

Recently I was in Israel and was again impressed with the beauty of the Holy City, Jerusalem. As tensions in the Mideast increase between the Arabs and the Israelis, I understand more and more why God commanded us to pray for the peace of Jerusalem. (Ps. 122:6.) But on this particular trip, I realized in a deeper way what lies behind the tensions and turmoil in the Holy Land: one ill-fated casualty covenant made thousands of years ago.

GOD'S PROMISE TO ABRAM

I traveled with a group of prayer intercessors across the entire nation of Israel, praying at religious sites and interceding for its leaders. Throughout this trip, I found my thoughts returning to Genesis, the Book of Beginnings, in which we meet Abram, a Chaldean from Ur.

God told Abram to leave his country and to go to the land He would show him. The Lord also gave Abram a promise:

**And I will make of thee a great nation,
and I will bless thee, and make thy name**

**great; and thou shalt be a blessing: and I
will bless them that bless thee, and curse
him that curseth thee: and in thee shall all
families of the earth be blessed.**

Genesis 12:2,3

The Lord had a plan for Abram to fulfill—a great part
in His divine purpose for the salvation of mankind.

So Abram obeyed the Lord. Taking his wife, Sarai, and
his relatives, he embarked on a journey toward Canaan.
Years later when Abram was dwelling in the land of
Canaan, God spoke to him again:

**And the Lord said unto Abram...Lift up
now thine eyes, and look from the place
where thou art northward, and southward,
and eastward, and westward: for all the
land which thou seest, to thee will I give it,
and to thy seed for ever. And I will make thy
seed as the dust of the earth: so that if a man
can number the dust of the earth, then shall
thy seed also be numbered.**

**Arise, walk through the land in the
length of it and in the breadth of it; for I will
give it unto thee.**

Genesis 13:14-17

Abram received specific divine instruction about the
land God had given him! We wonder how then things
have gone so awry over the centuries. Since that time,
there has been almost constant turmoil in the Holy Land,
and today Israel is a small nation in the midst of many
hostile nations. The turmoil continues.

The Arabs and the Jews disagree over their inheritance from their father Abraham (the name God gave Abram as part of the promise). This disagreement lies at the root of the existing conflict. On this trip to Israel, I saw the conflict with my heart as well as my eyes.

God's Word assures us that the blessings promised to the seed of Abraham apply not only to the physical realm but also to the spiritual realm. In other words, God's promise was not just for the descendants of Abraham but also for those of the same faith for all generations.

Whoever walks in God's way is also a child of the promise. Abraham was the father of *all* believers—those who accept Jesus Christ as the Messiah. (Rom. 4:11-13.) Therefore, God's promise to Abraham is a blessing that is available to all the people of the world.

THE CASUALTY COVENANT THAT SHOOK THE WORLD
• • •

Scripture tells us that Abram was the head of a large tribe of men and their families. There must have been a lot of laughing children in their tents, running and playing around the long skirts of their mothers.

Abram desired children as well. He believed that the Lord had promised him seed from his own body and that his seed would be as numerous as the stars. (Gen. 15:4-6.)

But although Abram was very rich in cattle, silver and gold (Gen. 13:2), he had no children of his own. Sarai, Abram's wife, was very beautiful and ten years younger than her husband, but she was barren.

In biblical days, barrenness was considered an affliction. Can you imagine the pain this condition brought to Sarai? Each month she hoped that she would find herself pregnant, but each month brought only fresh disappointment.

Sarai watched other women nursing their babies and holding children in their arms. She ached with longing to have a child of her own.

As she watched from her tent door, she must have pleaded with God, "Please give us a child to cherish, love and hold. Abram so wants a son. He believes that son will come from his own seed. Oh, God, hear my prayer!"

This prayer might have been followed with the wail, "Why, God? Why am I barren?" It seemed that only the wind heard her cry. God did not answer.

You can imagine how much her intense envy of the pregnant women in the camp tormented Sarai. Fearing she would always be barren, she began to entertain thoughts of using another woman, a surrogate, to conceive Abram's seed. She tried to brush these thoughts away, but they persisted like flies buzzing around her head.

I imagine that during one of these grievous, tormenting attacks, a dark, cruel figure waited in the wings, overseeing the assault. He watched her, goading her with accusations, filling her with desperate thoughts. He waited because he knew that desperate people can make desperate decisions.

Suddenly, the sinister figure moved. The moment to destroy God's plan for Abram and the Holy Land had come. He stood behind Sarai, invisible to her. His first plan was to infiltrate Sarai's thoughts with deceptive reasoning. Her desperation to have a baby made her vulnerable to his suggestion.

As Sarai's tears flowed, the evil spirit spoke to her, saying, *Hasn't God promised Abram that he will have a child from his own seed? But you are barren.*

Sarai had to agree that this was true. She was surprised at the next clear thought presented to her: *Then you can't deny your husband a child because you are barren. Why not give Abram your Egyptian handmaid, Hagar, and obtain children by her?*

As startling as the thought was to Sarai, it did seem to be a solution to her painful problem.

As she thought more and more on this proposition, it seemed to be the only solution that eased the aching in her heart. Obviously, Sarai didn't have a clue that Satan had hatched this scheme to wreak havoc with God's plan.

The devil had hit Sarai with doubt and unbelief at her weakest point: her capacity to bear a child. So she reasoned that she would help God out. By taking matters into her own hands, she gave Satan the green light to draw up a contract, a covenant, for a casualty!

Abram could have refused, but Scripture tells us that **Abram hearkened to the voice of Sarai** (Gen. 16:2). So Sarai gave Hagar to Abram, and he made her his wife. (v. 3.)

This situation has all the ingredients of a casualty covenant. And although Abram and Sarai were ignorant of Satan's scheme, the results of this false covenant were cataclysmic!

CASUALTY COVENANT CONSEQUENCES
· · ·

Of course, more problems developed. Hagar did conceive and immediately began to despise Sarai, causing Sarai to complain to Abram. Abram told her to take care of the matter herself, which Sarai did by dealing severely with Hagar.

Fleeing from Sarai, Hagar stopped by a spring of water in the wilderness. It was here that the angel of the Lord found her and gave her a divine message: She was to return to her mistress and submit to her control. The angel of the Lord also said to her:

> **I will multiply your descendants exceedingly so that they shall not be numbered for multitude....**
>
> **You are with child, and shall bear a son, and shall call his name Ishmael.... And he [Ishmael] will be as a wild ass among men; his hand will be against every man and every man's hand against him, and he will live to the east and on the borders of all his kinsmen.**
>
> **Genesis 16:10-12 AMP**

These Scriptures describe the life of the descendants of Ishmael, the Arabs of today.

Centuries of continual strife between the Arabs and Jews indicate the presence of a malignant, malevolent spiritual entity behind the scenes that has always sought to destroy Israel. Satan doesn't know everything, but he does know of his demise prophesied in the Bible. He also knows about God's plan for Jerusalem as the prophet Isaiah describes:

The sons of those who oppressed you shall come bending low to you; and all who despised you shall bow down at your feet; they shall call you the City of the Lord, the Zion of the Holy One of Israel.

Isaiah 60:14 RSV

Satan will do anything to keep that Scripture from coming to pass, including using the deception of casualty covenants!

ISAAC, THE PROMISED SON

. . .

The Lord saw all that had transpired in the lives of Hagar the bondwoman, Sarai the barren woman and Abram, with whom He was in covenant agreement.

When Abram was ninety-nine years old, the Lord appeared to him and said:

I am the Almighty God; walk before me, and be thou perfect. And I will make my covenant between me and thee, and will multiply thee exceedingly.

And Abram fell on his face: and God talked with him, saying, As for me, behold, my covenant is with thee, and thou shalt be a father of many nations. Neither shall thy name any more be called Abram, but thy name shall be Abraham; for a father of many nations have I made thee. And I will make thee exceeding fruitful, and I will make nations of thee, and kings shall come out of thee.

> **And I will establish my covenant between
> me and thee and thy seed after thee in their
> generations for an everlasting covenant, to
> be a God unto thee, and to thy seed after thee.
> And I will give unto thee, and to thy seed after
> thee, the land wherein thou art a stranger, all
> the land of Canaan, for an everlasting posses-
> sion; and I will be their God.**
>
> **Genesis 17:1-8**

When the Lord gave Abraham a new name, He also
changed Sarai's name to Sarah. God said He would give
her a son and bless her as a mother of many nations.

You can just imagine how shocked Abraham must
have been when he heard the news! **The Bible says he
fell on his face and laughed, and said to himself,
"Shall a child be born to a man who is a hundred
years old? Shall Sarah, who is ninety years old,
bear a child?"** (Gen. 17:17 RSV).

We can see from verse 18 that Abraham truly loved
Ishmael. He appealed to God, saying, **"O that Ishmael
might live in thy sight!"** (RSV).

God told Abraham that Ishmael would be fruitful and
multiply and become a great nation. But God said it
would be with Abraham and *Sarah's* son Isaac that He
would establish an everlasting covenant.

The Lord appeared to Abraham another time and
said that Sarah would bear a son in due season. Sarah
overheard this, and the Bible says that this time *she*
began to laugh. The Lord wanted to know why she
laughed. He asked her, *Is anything too hard or too
wonderful for the Lord?* (Gen. 18:14 AMP).

Both parents laughed at the thought of bearing a son in their old age. Thus, they named their son *Isaac*, which means "laughter."

At first, Sarah did not have enough faith to trust God to enable her to conceive. But later we are told in Hebrews 11:11:

Through faith also Sarah herself received strength to conceive seed, and was delivered of a child when she was past age, because she judged him faithful who had promised.

GOD'S PLAN *WILL* PREVAIL

Perhaps Sarah's casualty covenant delayed the fulfillment of God's promise to Abraham, but it did not stop it. Isaac was born, just as God promised. However, now there were two sons in the camp from the seed of Abraham: Ishmael from the bondwoman and Isaac from Sarah. Trouble always existed between the two sons and their mothers, so Hagar and Ishmael finally had to leave.

Abraham loved them both, but God said, **In Isaac shall thy seed be called. And also of the son of the bondwoman will I make a nation, because he is thy seed** (Gen. 21:12,13).

We know the rest of the story: continual striving and fighting between the Arabs and the Jews. The results of a casualty covenant made long ago planted bitter roots of hatred and jealousy in the hearts of two boys over the love of their father, Abraham. Their descendants continue to this day to war with one another.

Behind all this rebellion, the spirit of antichrist continually seeks to stir up strife in order to abort the plan of God. But as we pray for the peace of Jerusalem according to God's command, it will be His plan, His purposes and His everlasting covenant that will ultimately prevail to His promised seed!

14

BAD NEWS COVENANTS VS. THE GOOD NEWS COVENANT

As we discover the danger of casualty covenants, we become more alert in recognizing the strategies of the enemy. We know that Satan studies us, seeking to infiltrate our thought life with his lies so he can bring us into covenant agreement with him.

CHANGE YOUR THINKING PATTERNS

• • •

The more our understanding grows, the more we realize how strong a covenant agreement really is. We also come to realize that the conscious or unconscious casualty covenants we make with the enemy develop into strongholds in our souls. (2 Cor. 10:4.) These destructive thoughts travel like a swift locomotive, rushing us to distorted destinies, crafted by wrong decisions and wrong behavior. It is possible to escape such destinations—but only if we let our divine "conductor" switch the patterns of our thinking.

The enemy of our souls has put forth much effort and time to lay down his own evil "tracks" in our thoughts. These rails enable him to send a load of bad news and carnal thoughts to our brains whenever it serves his purpose. In essence, the devil has programmed us to think according to his own patterns of destruction and deceit.

Since Satan is sometimes able to lay the tracks of unhealthy thought patterns in our minds, he is well familiar with the lies that he's told us—and that we've accepted. So he knows how we will respond. When he wants to control a relationship or situation, he attacks us by riding those rails with negative thoughts that trigger damaged emotions and wrong actions.

This tangle of tumultuous thoughts is like a thicket. You feel entangled in darkness with no way out. This is the devil's deception because, for those in Christ, the Bible promises that there *is* a way out of desperate thoughts:

> **There hath no temptation taken you but such as is common to man: but God is faithful, who will not suffer you to be tempted above that ye are able; but will with the temptation also make a way to escape, that ye may be able to bear it.**
>
> **1 Corinthians 10:13**

Jesus Christ is the way out of the devilish lies that torment us and hold us in bondage. He gives us clear instruction on how to deal with those mental strongholds:

> **Casting down imaginations, and every high thing that exalteth itself against the**

knowledge of God, and bringing into captivity every thought to the obedience of Christ.

2 Corinthians 10:5

The enemy can control our thought processes more than we realize, so we must consistently cast down thoughts that are contrary to God's eternal Word and lay some scriptural tracks of our own. As we meditate on those Scriptures and lay those tracks, we can actually break those destructive thought patterns and increase in our obedience to God's Word, namely by thinking as God thinks.

For example, here are some excellent truths for us to fix our thoughts on:

Let the weak say, I am strong.

Joel 3:10

No weapon that is formed against thee shall prosper.

Isaiah 54:17

The Lord is my helper, and I will not fear what man shall do unto me.

Hebrews 13:6

HARMFUL COVENANTS

· · ·

We have a responsibility to renew our minds with God's written Word. Then we must confess His Word with our mouths instead of confessing the negative thoughts and words the devil gives us.

For instance, how many marriages are broken because of the word *divorce?* First it is just a fleeting thought. Then that unspoken word becomes a sentence. Finally it is a stronghold in the married couple's minds—only to end with the breaking of the couple's covenant bond.

Or how many precious people accept the lie that they are doomed in life by their genetic makeup? They never realize that our Creator's healing power is greater than any "defective" gene or trait a person could inherit!

Or how many noble Christians are conned through deceptive thoughts into making unconscious covenants with Satan to believe that their suffering somehow glorifies God? The truth is, suffering doesn't indicate any virtue on our part. Certainly, ignorance of God's Word is *not* a virtue. (God's Word tells us Jesus redeemed us from suffering.) Instead, it is an opportunity for our merciless enemy to attack.

The idea of suffering a physical disease for God's glory does not come from an honest appraisal of the Scriptures. You can be sure that if sickness glorifies God, then Jesus would not have healed the sick.

How God anointed Jesus of Nazareth with the Holy Ghost and with power: who went about doing good, and healing all that were oppressed of the devil; for God was with him.

Acts 10:38

Some have longed for death to come because of their broken hearts or physical pain. Others have died and had heavenly, supernatural experiences and desired to stay there.

Let's not make a covenant with a spirit of death before our time. Hebrews 9:27 says, **It is appointed**

unto men once **to die, and after this the judgment.**
Please note that this Scripture says, **It is appointed...
once to die.** It does not say *the time is appointed.* Let's
allow our Father God to call us home. He knows our
names, and He will send His holy angels for us. Let us
break any covenants we have ever made concerning
sickness and premature death right now in the name of
Jesus Christ.

God loves us; we are His creation. He is for us, not
against us. (Rom. 8:31.) He has made a covenant with us.
It is signed with the lifeblood of His dear Son.

When God made a covenant with mankind, He
extended His love to us. Although He is sovereign, He
has limited Himself to our decision of accepting His gift
of love wrapped up in the life of His Son.

God's Covenants
. . .

As we begin to study God's covenants, notice these
key Scriptures:

**For the law was given through Moses;
grace and truth came through Jesus Christ.**

John 1:17 NIV

The law was given to Moses (this is the Mosaic
Covenant), and it was a shadow of things to come. But
the substance of what was foreshadowed is in Christ.
(Col. 1:16.)

The Old Testament contains the old covenant, and
the New Testament contains our new covenant. And
what a covenant it is!

BREAKING CASUALTY COVENANTS

Jeremiah prophesied of the new covenant:

"Behold, days are coming," declares the Lord, "when I will make a new covenant with the house of Israel and with the house of Judah, not like the covenant which I made with their fathers in the day I took them by the hand to bring them out of the land of Egypt, My covenant which they broke, although I was a husband to them," declares the Lord.

"But this is the covenant which I will make with the house of Israel after those days," declares the Lord, "I will put My law within them, and on their heart I will write it; and I will be their God, and they shall be My people."

Jeremiah 31:31-33 NAS

When Jesus was eating His Last Supper, the Passover meal, with His disciples, **He took the cup after supper saying, This cup is the new testament or covenant [ratified] in My blood, which is shed (poured out) for you** (Luke 22:20 AMP).

God's own Son was the One who paid the price for mankind's sins and brought about the new covenant, enabling those who receive Him in faith to become heirs of God. This new covenant brings us into union with Him.

BENEFITS OF THE NEW COVENANT
• • •

When we receive Jesus into our hearts, we become spiritually united and commingled with God through the everlasting covenant—no matter where we are and what we are doing. Jesus is the Mediator of this new covenant. (Heb. 12:24.) It is sealed with His blood that He shed for us on Calvary's Cross.

So many benefits await believers in the new covenant. Above all, Jesus Christ died that we all might live eternally.

Forasmuch then as the children are partakers of flesh and blood, he also himself likewise took part of the same; that through death he might destroy him that had the power of death, that is, the devil.

Hebrews 2:14

Jesus also took our diseases that we might have health.

Who forgiveth all thine iniquities; who healeth all thy diseases.

Psalm 103:3

He took our poverty as well that we might have wealth.

For ye know the grace of our Lord Jesus Christ, that, though he was rich, yet for your sakes he became poor, that ye through his poverty might be rich.

2 Corinthians 8:9

Psalm 84:11 becomes ours to claim:

The Lord will give grace and glory: no good thing will he withhold from them that walk uprightly.

When tests and trials come, we are not alone.

Ye are of God, little children, and have overcome them: because greater is he that is in you, than he that is in the world.

1 John 4:4

Through the Holy Spirit, who authored the Holy Word, we have been given access to the gifts of the Spirit. (1 Cor. 12:7-11.) The comfort and counsel of the same Holy Spirit are also ours through Jesus Christ.

But the Comforter, which is the Holy Ghost, whom the Father will send in my name, he shall teach you all things, and bring all things to your remembrance, whatsoever I [Jesus] have said unto you.

John 14:26

We can receive the Lord's peace in the most trying circumstances:

Peace I leave with you, my peace I give unto you: not as the world giveth, give I unto you. Let not your heart be troubled, neither let it be afraid.

John 14:27

We can also have an immediate audience with Almighty God through prayer in Jesus' name. What a deal this new covenant is! Let us accept His help. He tells us,

Let us therefore come boldly unto the throne of grace, that we may obtain mercy, and find grace to help in time of need.

Hebrews 4:16

And according to 1 John 2:1-2, we don't have to approach the throne of grace alone:

We have an advocate [lawyer] **with the Father, Jesus Christ the righteous: and he is the propitiation** [One who makes atonement] **for our sins: and not for ours only, but also for the sins of the whole world.**

To enjoy all these benefits of our covenant with God, we must first fulfill Romans 6:11,14:

Reckon ye also yourselves to be dead indeed unto sin, but alive unto God through Jesus Christ our Lord.

For sin shall not have dominion over you: for ye are not under the law, but under grace.

Then we will reign with Him:

For if by one man's [Adam's] **offence death reigned by one; much more they which receive abundance of grace and of the gift of righteousness shall reign in life by one, Jesus Christ.**

Romans 5:17

In all these things we are more than conquerors through him that loved us.

Romans 8:37

Jesus is our victory—when we let Him live His victorious life through us. The Christian life is impossible to live by our own human efforts, but it becomes enjoyable when we yield to Jesus' nature, letting His life flow through us. We can have the mind of Christ. (1 Cor. 2:16.) We can be **strengthened with all might, according to his glorious power, unto all patience and longsuffering with joyfulness** (Col. 1:11).

We are called to be kings and priests in the kingdom of heaven. (Rev. 1:6.) We will share the inheritance of the Lord Jesus Christ.

> **Praised (honored, blessed) be the God and Father of our Lord Jesus Christ (the Messiah)! By His boundless mercy we have been born again to an ever-living hope through the resurrection of Jesus Christ from the dead. [Born anew] into an inheritance which is beyond the reach of change and decay (imperishable), unsullied, and unfading, reserved in heaven for you.**
>
> **1 Peter 1:3,4** AMP

> **Giving thanks to the Father, who has qualified and made us fit to share the portion which is the inheritance of the saints (God's holy people) in the Light.**
>
> **Colossians 1:12** AMP

We are to be conformed to the image of God's Son, possessing His character and nature of love, joy and peace. (Rom. 8:29.) We are called to be winners, not losers. (Deut. 28:13.)

In ways that are more than we can think, ask or imagine, *Christians are the beneficiaries of the new covenant.*

In the face of such a wonderful covenant, the only tool Satan has to use against mankind is deception. He uses fear, intimidation, flattery and condemnation—whatever it takes to capture humans for his control.

We have all been duped at one time or another by the devil's devious devices. But we can escape his snares by resisting his lies and choosing God's truth. *The choice is ours.*

ENTER INTO COVENANT WITH GOD
. . .

Are you a covenant man or woman? Would you like to be? Would you like to receive Jesus into your heart? All you have to do is ask Him to forgive you of your sins and invite Him into your heart. You, too, can be a partaker of the blessings of His new covenant. This is the most important decision you will ever make—choosing life eternal for your eternal spirit.

There is no middle ground. Satan hates you and uses lies to destroy you. God loves you and wants you to have eternal life with Him. Therefore, allow God to make you whole in your spirit, your soul and your body.

Will you accept God's holy covenant for yourself today? *Will you say yes to Jesus?*

I assure you, *this* is the covenant to make.

Let us pray:

> *Lord Jesus, forgive me of my sins. I accept that You died on the Cross for my sins, were buried and then arose from the grave. Thank You for loving me enough to die for me. I invite You, King of kings and Lord of lords, into my heart. Thank You for my salvation, which You have provided through Your shed blood on the Cross. Amen.*

Now this is my prayer in Ephesians 3:16-19 for you:

That he would grant you, according to the riches of his glory, to be strengthened

with might by his Spirit in the inner man;
that Christ may dwell in your hearts by
faith; that ye, being rooted and grounded in
love, may be able to comprehend with all
saints what is the breadth, and length, and
depth, and height; and to know the love of
Christ, which passeth knowledge, that ye
might be filled with all the fulness of God.

Amen.

ENDNOTES

Chapter 1

[1] *Webster's New World College Dictionary*, 3d College Ed., s.v. "covenant."

Chapter 2

[1] Scofield, Ref. 3d Ed., Note 1, p. 1270.

[2] Nee, *The Spiritual Man*, Volume III, p. 59.

Chapter 3

[1] Gee, p. 22.

[2] Elliott. "Just as I Am."

Chapter 4

[1] Solomon, p. 45.

[2] Sumrall, p. 5.

[3] Solomon, p. 35.

[4] Meyer, p. 25.

[5] Hammond, pp. 8-9, 46.

[6] Hammond, p. 29.

[7] Wilcox, p. 86.

[8] Elliott, p. 78.

Chapter 5

[1] Liardon, p. 82.

[2] Liardon, pp. 58-59.

[3] Ibid.

[4] Hoch, p. 249.

[5] Pollard, Adelaide and George C. Stebbins. "Have Thine Own Way, Lord."

[6] Beattie, p. 189.

[7] Chisholm, Thomas O. and William M. Runyan. "Great Is Thy Faithfulness."

[8] Bobgan, p. 35-36.

[9] Bobgan, p. 43.

Chapter 6

[1] Hart, p. 7.

[2] Cherry, p. 11.

[3] Cho, Vol. 1, p. 169. Permission for reproducing this testimony was granted by Dr. (Paul) David Yonggi Cho on March 23, 1993.

[4] Cho, Vol. 2, pp. xii-xviii.

[5] Cho, Vol. 1, pp. 169-171.

[6] Malz, p. 168.

Chapter 7

[1] Curran, p. 69.

[2] "You think you have stress? Think about Mafia." *The Houston Post,* July 11, 1989.

[3] ten Boom, pp. 52-54.

[4] *The World Book Encyclopedia,* Vol. 19, p. 410.

[5] Harries, p. 475-77.

[6] Harries, p. 456.

[7] Hitt, p. 224.

[8] Ibid, pp. 224-26.

[9] Ibid, pp. 226-27.

[10] Ibid, p. 227-28.

[11] Ibid, p. 228-29.

[12] Sarah F. Adams. "Nearer My God, to Thee."

[13] Rankin, Jeremiah E. "God Be With You."

Chapter 8

[1] Traditional. "He Is Lord."

Chapter 9

[1] Nee, *The Spiritual Man, Vol. 3,* pp. 21-25, 29.

[2] Mumford, p. 87.

Chapter 11

[1] Hagin, p. 99.

[2] *Webster's New World College Dictionary,* 3d College Ed., s.v. "to occupy."

Chapter 12

[1] Wagner, p. 79.

[2] Nee, *The Latent Power of the Soul,* p. 46-47.

REFERENCES

Adams, Sarah F. "Nearer, My God to Thee." *The Lutheran Hymnal*. St. Louis: Concordia Publishing House, 1941.

Beattie, Melody. *The Language of Letting Go*. Center City: Hazelden Foundation, 1990.

Bobgan, Martin and Diedre. *Hypnosis and the Christian*. Minneapolis: Bethany House Publishers, 1984.

Cherry, Reginald, M.D. *The Bible Cure*. Lake Mary: Creation House, 1996.

Chisholm, Thomas O. "Great Is Thy Faithfulness." *The Baptist Hymnal*. Carol Stream: Hope Publishing Company, 1951.

Cho, David Yonggi. *The Fourth Dimension*. New Jersey: Logos International, 1979.

Cho, David Yonggi and Whitney Manzano, Ph.D. *The Fourth Dimension, Volume Two*. New Jersey: Logos International, 1979.

Curran, Sue. *The Forgiving Church*. Blountville: Shekinah Publishers, 1990.

Elliott, Charlotte. "Just as I Am." *Hymns, Psalms, and Spiritual Songs*. Westminster Press, 1950.

Elliott, William M. *The Cure for Anxiety*. Richmond: John Knox Press, 1964.

Gee, Donald. *Temptations of the Spirit-filled Christ*. Springfield: Gospel Publishing House, 1966.

Hagin, Kenneth E. *The Holy Spirit and His Gifts*. Tulsa: Kenneth Hagin Ministries, Inc., 1991.

Hammond, Frank D. *Overcoming Rejection*. Kirkwood: Impact Christian Books, Inc., 1987.

Hart, Archibald. *Adrenaline and Stress*. Pasadena: Word Publishing, 1991.

Harries, Merion and Susie. *Prisoners of the Sun*. New York: Random House Publisher, 1994.

"He Is Lord." *Songs for Praise and Worship*. Nashville: Word Music, 1986.

Hitt, Russell T. *Sensei*. New York: Harper and Row Publishers, 1965.

Hoch, Edward Wallis."Good and Bad." *The Oxford Dictionary of Quotations.* 2d Ed. London: Oxford University Press, 1953.

Liardon, Roberts. *Breaking Controlling Powers.* Tulsa: Harrison House, 1988.

Malz, Betty. *Prayers That Are Answered.* Lincoln: Chosen Books, 1980.

Meyer, Joyce. *The Root of Rejection.* Tulsa: Harrison House, 1994.

Mumford, Bob. *Take Another Look at Guidance.* Raleigh: Lifechangers Publishing, 1971.

Nee, Watchman. *The Latent Power of the Soul.* New York: Christian Fellowship Publishers, Inc., 1972. Used by permission.

Nee, Watchman. *The Spiritual Man, Vol. III.* New York: Christian Fellowship Publishers, Inc., 1968.

Pollard, Adelaide and George C. Stebbins. "Have Thine Own Way, Lord." *The Baptist Hymnal.* Carol Stream: Hope Publishing Company, 1951.

Rankin, Jeremiah E. "God Be With You." *Favorite Hymns of Praise.* Wheaton: Tabernacle Publishing Co., 1967.

Solomon, Charles R. *The Ins and out of Rejection.* Sevierville: Solomon Publications, 1976.

Sumrall, Lester. *How To Cope Series: Rejection.* Tulsa: Harrison House, 1983.

ten Boom, Corrie. *Marching Orders for the End Battle.* Fort Washington: Christian Literature Crusade, 1969.

The Scofield Reference Bible. Ref. 3d Ed. C.T. Scofield, Ed. New York: Oxford University Press, 1945.

The World Book Encyclopedia. Vol. 19. Chicago: World Book Publishing, 1962.

Wagner, C. Peter. W*arfare Prayer.* Ventura: Regal Books, 1992.

Webster's New World College Dictionary. 3d College Ed. New York: Macmillan General Reference, 1986.

Wilcox, Ella Wheeler. "New Year Resolve." *Kingdom of Love and How Salvator Won.* Chicago: W. B. Conkey Company, 1902.

ABOUT THE AUTHOR

Mickie Winborn is the wife of Kenneth E. Winborn. Mickie and Kenneth were both raised in Houston, Texas, where they joined the Methodist church shortly after their wedding. They are the parents of two sons and grandparents of five.

When her sons were young, Mickie held weekly Bible classes for the neighborhood children in her home. At that time, she also served on the board of The Women's Christian Home in Houston, helping hurting women regain control of their lives. She now serves with the auxiliary for The Women's Home. She also serves on the advisory board of Joysprings Foundation, Inc. of Franklin Springs, Georgia.

Mickie is an ordained minister and is the president of Mickie Winborn Ministries, Inc. In 1976 she founded Prayer Bible Studies of Houston for Catholic women who desired to study the Bible. She continues to teach this group, which currently meets monthly and has expanded into an inter-denominational membership of men and women.

In the 1980s, Mickie ministered in workshops on various college campuses with the National Convocation of Christian Leaders, sponsored by Fuller Theological Seminary and the Lowell Berry Foundation.

She has appeared on many Christian and secular television programs sharing about her miraculous healing or terminal cancer. She also ministers regularly in healing services for different organizations and churches in which the Lord confirms His Word with signs and wonders.

Mickie has ministered in miracle services in Hong Kong, Panama, Costa Rica and extensively in the United States. In these meetings, tumors have fallen off, cancer has been healed, the handicapped have walked out of wheelchairs, backs and limbs have been healed, eyes have been healed and all manner of diseases have been cured. Creative miracles have been visibly manifested—such as arches appearing in feet and the deaf and mute hearing and speaking.

Mickie has ministered in Haiti, being invited to the palace for an audience with the ruler's mother. She has also been a speaker on cruise ships to many different countries.

In addition, Mickie has served since the early nineties as a prayer intercessor for several international groups. She has been to South Korea twice with the Spiritual Warfare Network, serving as a prayer leader there and in conferences in the United States. She is a personal intercessor for C. Peter Wagner, President of World Prayer Center and for others who are involved in that exciting ministry to the world.

Mickie also speaks at retreats and particularly likes speaking to college students. Recently, she and her grown granddaughter, who is a missionary, joined an intercessor's prayer tour to Israel, where they prayed with different leaders in the country.

To contact Mickie Winborn,
write:

Mickie Winborn Ministries, Inc.
P.O. Box 19194
Houston, TX 77024

OTHER BOOKS BY
MICKIE WINBORN

Through a Glass, Darkly

Available from your local bookstore

Additional copies of this book
Are available from your local bookstore.

HARRISON HOUSE
Tulsa, Oklahoma 74153

THE HARRISON HOUSE VISION

Proclaiming the truth and the power
Of the Gospel of Jesus Christ
With excellence;

Challenging Christians to
Live victoriously,
Grow spiritually,
Know God intimately.